D1548992

OFFICIAL GUIDE
TO THE

NATIONAL MUSEUM
OF
AMERICAN HISTORY

The Foucault pendulum gives a visual demonstration of the rotation of the earth.

OFFICIAL GUIDE
TO THE

NATIONAL MUSEUM

OF

AMERICAN HISTORY

Published for the National Museum of American History

by the
Smithsonian Institution Press
Washington, D.C.

Library of Congress Cataloging-in-Publication Data

National Museum of American History (U.S.)
  Guidebook to the National Museum of American History.

  1. National Museum of American History (U.S.)—Guide-books.   I. Title.
E172.N3826 1990 973'.074013 87-600337
ISBN 0-87474-683-3

Cover photo: Star-Spangled Banner. This is the flag that flew over Fort McHenry during the attack of the British fleet in 1814 and inspired Francis Scott Key to write the poem that became the words to our national anthem.

Guidebook Staff
R.D. Selim, *Writer and Project Coordinator*
Eric Long, Jeff Tinsley, Dane Penland, Laurie Minor, Richard Strauss, Kim Nielsen, Richard Hofmeister, Jeffrey Ploskonka, *Photographers*

Sincere thanks to the following people for their invaluable help in preparing this guidebook: Alan Carter, Paula Dailey, Ann Dargis, Heidi Lumberg, Caroline Newman, Suzanne Hastings, Rita Adrosko, Sheila Alexander, David Allison, Sandra Babbidge, Charlene Barnard, Reggie Blaszczyk, Joan Boudreau, Deborah Bretzfelder, Nancy Brooks, Jim Bruns, Betty Burch, J. Michael Carrigan, Elvira Clain-Stefanelli, Claudine Klose, Harold Closter, Herbert Collins, Tom Crouch, Pete Daniel, Jon Eklund, Ed Ezell, John Fesperman, Barney Finn, Paul Forman, Susan Foster, Cory Gillilland, Donna Green, Rayna Green, Rob Harding, Michael Harris, Elizabeth Harris, Ellen Roney Hughes, Roger Kennedy, Don Kloster, Ray Kondratas, Joyce Lancaster, Harold Langley, Peter Liebhold, Steve Lubar, Art Molella, Susan Myers, Richard Nicastro, George Norton, Eugene Ostroff, Robert Post, Charles Rand, Carl Scheele, Barbara Clark Smith, Carlene Stephens, Mary Stewart, John Stine, Gary Sturm, Lonn Taylor, William Tompkins, Lois Vann, Margaret Vining, Robert Vogel, Lynne Vosloh, Jim Wallace, Deborah Warner, Roger White, John White, William Withuhn, Helena Wright, Janice Wheeler, Marie Carter, Spencer Crew.

CONTENTS

WELCOME TO THE NATIONAL MUSEUM OF AMERICAN HISTORY

At the National Museum of American History we preserve tangible pieces of history—correspondence, tools, automobiles, sheet music, cyclotrons, gowns, flags, and countless other survivors of the past—as the past itself slips away. We also attempt to reconstruct more elusive pieces of the past, through music, drama, and the oral heritage of Americans. Curators and other scholars analyze all these fragments, seeking to reconstruct larger portions of the whole and to find meaningful patterns that will increase our understanding of our history and ourselves. We present these patterns to our visitors through exhibitions, publications, and public programs.

This work involves the labors of many people, including scores of volunteers. Along with our curatorial divisions, we have offices of public programs, conservation, exhibits design and production, registrar, collections management, computer services, security, and public affairs, to name a few, as well as two libraries and an Archives Center. The breadth of the expert knowledge in the Museum testifies to the magnitude of our mission. It is to collect, preserve, exhibit, interpret, and honor the heritage of the American people.

Many visitors still think of this building as the Museum of History and Technology, the name under which it opened in 1964. But in 1980 the name was changed to the National Museum of American History to more accurately reflect the scope of our interests and responsibilities.

Roger Kennedy
Director, National Museum of American History

ABOUT THE MUSEUM
AND THIS GUIDE

This guide describes the Museum from the first floor up, but you need not visit it that way. Let your interests lead you. If you enter any hall in the Museum and see something that fascinates you, chances are you will be able to find out a good deal more about it right there, within a few steps in one direction or another, or somewhere else in the building.

A few important things to remember:

• Only a fraction of the more than 18 million objects in the Museum's collections are on display. Some of the objects mentioned or illustrated in this guide may not be exhibited during your visit. Many others not described here will be on display.

• The descriptions of the exhibitions in this guide are far from complete. The guide outlines the major themes and sections of exhibitions and gives a glimpse of the objects inside. If you really want to know what's in a hall, you have to see it for yourself.

• The floor plans show several galleries for temporary exhibitions, which are not described here. Ask about temporary exhibitions at the information desks.

• Almost every major exhibition hall has galleries or areas designed for changing exhibits. Like temporary exhibitions, these are not described in this guide.

• The Museum is undergoing extensive renovations and reinstallations of its permanent exhibitions in the 1990s. Some exhibitions that have been here since the Museum opened its doors in 1964 have changed already, and others will change over the next several years.

NATIONAL MUSEUM OF AMERICAN HISTORY

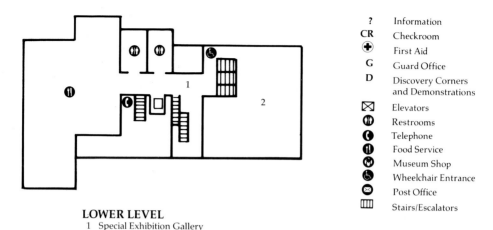

?	Information
CR	Checkroom
✚	First Aid
G	Guard Office
D	Discovery Corners and Demonstrations
⊠	Elevators
🚻	Restrooms
☎	Telephone
🍴	Food Service
🛍	Museum Shop
♿	Wheelchair Entrance
✉	Post Office
▥	Stairs/Escalators

LOWER LEVEL
1 Special Exhibition Gallery
2 Museum Shop/Bookstore

FIRST FLOOR

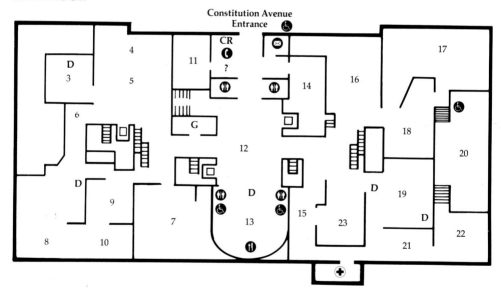

3 Textiles
4 Atomic Clocks
5 Atom Smashers
6 Special Exhibition Gallery
7 Dibner Library
8 Medical Sciences
9 Special Exhibition Gallery
10 Physical Sciences
11 Special Exhibition Gallery
12 A Material World
13 The Palm Court

14 Auditorium
15 Timekeeping
16 Agriculture
17 American Maritime Enterprise
18 Road Transportation
19 Electricity
20 Railroads
21 Power Machinery
22 Bridges & Tunnels
23 Engines of Change

NATIONAL MUSEUM OF AMERICAN HISTORY

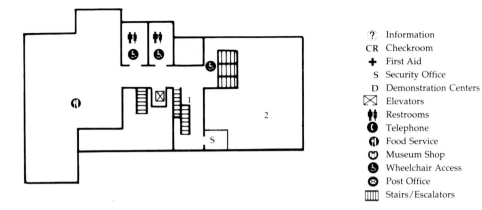

?	Information
CR	Checkroom
+	First Aid
S	Security Office
D	Demonstration Centers
⊠	Elevators
♰♰	Restrooms
☎	Telephone
🍴	Food Service
🛍	Museum Shop
♿	Wheelchair Access
✉	Post Office
⫴⫴	Stairs/Escalators

LOWER LEVEL
1 Special Exhibition Gallery
2 Museum Shop/Bookstore

FIRST FLOOR

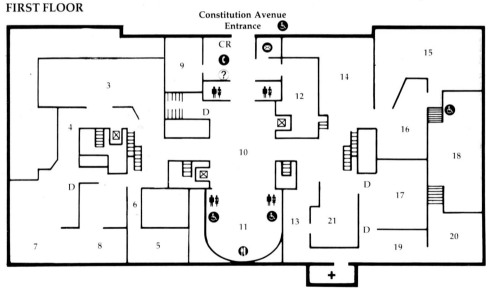

3	Information Age	12	Carmichael Auditorium
4	Special Exhibition Gallery	13	Timekeeping
5	Dibner Library	14	Agriculture
6	Dibner Gallery	15	American Maritime Enterprise
7	Medical Sciences	16	Road Transportation
8	Physical Sciences	17	Electricity
9	Special Exhibition Gallery	18	Railroads
10	A Material World	19	Power Machinery
11	The Palm Court	20	Bridges and Tunnels
		21	Engines of Change

SECOND FLOOR

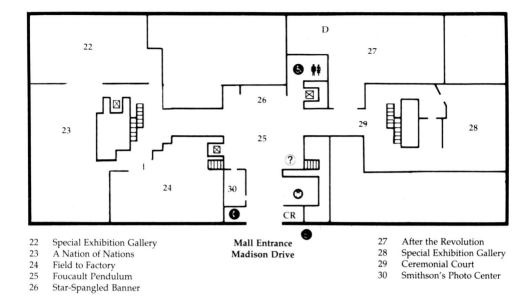

22	Special Exhibition Gallery	
23	A Nation of Nations	
24	Field to Factory	
25	Foucault Pendulum	
26	Star-Spangled Banner	

Mall Entrance
Madison Drive

27	After the Revolution
28	Special Exhibition Gallery
29	Ceremonial Court
30	Smithson's Photo Center

THIRD FLOOR

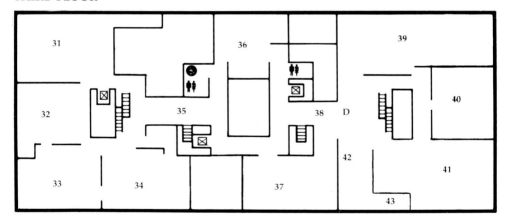

31	Ceramics
32	Musical Instruments
33	Philately and Postal History
34	Printing and Graphic Arts
35	Textiles

36	Money and Medals
37	Photography
38	Special Exhibition Gallery
39	Armed Forces
40	Archives Center
41	A More Perfect Union
42	Gunboat *Philadelphia*
43	Firearms Gallery

This insert reflects the 1991 configuration of the Museum's exhibition areas. For up-to-date information on changing installations and special exhibitions, please ask at the information desks.

SECOND FLOOR

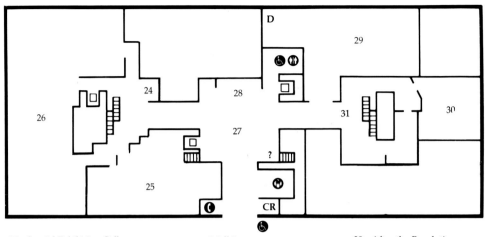

24	Special Exhibition Gallery	**Mall Entrance**	29 After the Revolution
25	Special Exhibition Gallery		30 Special Exhibition Gallery
26	A Nation of Nations	**Madison Drive**	31 Ceremonial Court
27	Foucault Pendulum		
28	Star-Spangled Banner		

THIRD FLOOR

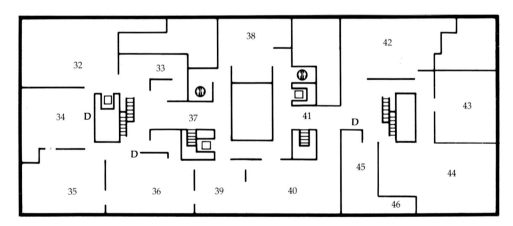

32 Ceramics
33 Glass
34 Musical Instruments
35 Philately & Postal History
36 Printing & Graphic Arts
37 Special Exhibition Gallery

38 Money & Medals
39 News Reporting
40 Photography
41 Special Exhibition Gallery
42 Armed Forces
43 Archives Center
44 A More Perfect Union
45 Gunboat Philadelphia
46 Firearms Gallery

This early 19th-century spinning wheel for wool is made of ash and maple. Until the mid-19th century, most mechanisms in America were made of wood.

THE EXHIBITIONS

FIRST FLOOR

A Material World

This exhibition asks a simple question of the artifacts it contains and indirectly of every "thing" in the Museum and anywhere else: "What is it made of?" *A Material World* is about both seeing and doing, discovering the inner structure of the materials around us and using the discoveries to forge those materials into new shapes, new tools, new machines.

In the course of American history, the use of various materials changed as a result of a complex set of factors: the depletion of some natural resources, new methods for processing materials, and changes in taste and fashion. When the United States was largely a nation of independent farmers, the predominant materials were those that required little modification from their natural state—slate and stone, cotton, wool, leather, grasses, and especially wood.

Industrialization brought to the fore materials that required more energy and new kinds of skill to process, notably in the arcane art and science of metallurgy. Now, in the post-industrial age, many of our materials are synthesized from liquid and gaseous resources through chemical processes even more complex and energy-intensive. A "Materials Panorama" explores the nature and uses of these three broad classes of materials by showing the "raw" materials themselves and the objects they came to be.

Grasses, hides, stone, and wood were among the most important raw materials early Americans, both native and newly arrived from Europe, used to build the world they lived in. Among Euro-Americans, wood was preeminent among these materials. Indeed, a "wooden age" in American history lasted for some 200 years until the mid-19th century. The first part of the panorama presents timbers, bricks, plaster, cowhide, slate, and

This cast-aluminum observation-car sign was designed in 1938 by Henry Dreyfuss for the 20th Century Limited *train. When scientists first learned to make aluminum in the laboratory in the 19th century, they called it "silver from clay."*

other materials to give a broad view of natural materials. These "raw" materials are displayed with artifacts they were fashioned into, including a backstaff from 1769, a powder horn of 1795, a whale-oil lamp of the 1820s, a tower-clock mechanism of the 1830s, a spinning wheel of about 1840, a wampum belt of the 1850s, even 1880s puppets.

As the pace of industrialization quickened after the 1830s, Americans began to form their world more of metal—first iron and later steel. The "Materials Panorama" introduces this new age in samples of cast-iron for forging, rolled steel plates, pressed tin, steel-reinforced concrete, sheet steel, and other materials. The objects shown include an 1841 parlor stove, hand tools of the 1850s, a railroad lantern of 1865, a sewing machine of 1877, a time lock of the 1880s, and a steam pump of the 1890s. Special exhibits along the way highlight the importance of new methods of making steel, a machine for drawing sheet steel, and a test section of cable for the George Washington Bridge, made in 1929.

A third section of the "Materials Panorama" looks at aluminum and alloy steels and at the world of synthetics, from the first, celluloid and Bakelite, to the most recent, such as Kevlar. Samples of aluminum, stainless steel, nylon, glass-reinforced polyester, acrylic, and other materials provide a setting for objects such as an erector set made about 1913, an aluminum sign of the 1930s for the

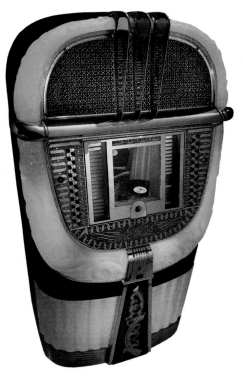

Jukeboxes like this 1946 AMI Model A were a celebration of the qualities inherent in plastics: translucency, colorability, and moldability— the very quality of "plasticity."

20th Century Limited train, an acrylic and chrome-plated jukebox from 1946, a record-setting bicycle, and an artificial heart.

Squeeze this panorama of "modern" materials into a single machine and what have you got? Possibly a swamp rat. The Swamp Rat XXX, a top-fuel dragster designed and built by Don Garlits in 1986, is a symphony of modern materials; more than four dozen, from chrome-moly steel to a Kevlar-carbon fiber composite, went into its making.

Here the exhibition delves deeper into new materials: their origins, special properties, early applications, rise to popularity, and in some cases slide into disuse. Exhibits on the dragster, including a dramatic videotape showing a crash at well over 200 miles per hour, demonstrate the great strength of its component materials. Railroad rails, turbine blades, and a crankshaft of "Kryptonite"—in a sense the ultimate material—help explain the uses and properties of alloy steels. The history of aluminum takes on three dimensions in jewelry, kitchenware, a baseball bat, an engine block of the 1980s, even a violin. Objects made wholly or largely of celluloid include film, cuffs and collars, and a billiard ball. Jewelry, electrical components, and a dashboard are among the Bakelite artifacts.

In the final section of *A Material World,* groups of the same object made of different materials offer an opportunity to contemplate the differences in materials, their abundance and scarcity, and the tastes and fash-

Don Garlits's Swamp Rat XXX in action. This top-fuel dragster is a symphony of synthetics, particularly alloy steels; lightweight alloys using aluminum, magnesium, and titanium; elastomeric and hard polymers; and composites of polymers and fibers.

ions of a culture that would prefer, say, a plastic chair to a wooden one. Here are a wooden Windsor chair of the 1790s and a molded acrylic chair of the 1960s; helmets from leather to steel to plastic; wooden, aluminum, and carbon-fiber tennis rackets; and many other like objects set side by side to display the contrasts among the materials they are made of.

Engines of Change: The American Industrial Revolution, 1790–1860
In the early 19th century, new machines, new sources of power, and new ways of organizing work transformed the United States from an agricultural nation to an industrial power. *Engines of Change: The American Industrial Revolution, 1790–1860,* in the east wing of the first floor, introduces some of the people and machines that were part of this great transformation. In *Engines of Change* some of the most important machines of the American Industrial Revolution are displayed as part of the history of their times.

The exhibition begins with American machines and products of the early 19th century—including the McCormick reaper and a Chickering piano—in a re-creation of the 1851 London "Crystal Palace" World's Fair, where American technology first won international recognition. The exhibition then moves back to 1790 to examine the circumstances that made the American triumph at the Crystal Palace possible. A piece of a sawmill from Chester County, Pennsylvania,

The acrylic Lily Chair of 1959, designed by Erwine and Estelle Laverne, was made "invisible" to make the person seated in it more visible.

14

Before the Industrial Revolution, 9 out of 10 Americans lived on farms and used a variety of tools and machines in their everyday work. A tradition of mechanical ingenuity and self-reliance in the United States helped the Industrial Revolution flourish here.

Americans were pioneers in wood technology. These gears are made of five different species of wood, an example of how well American craftsmen understood the strengths and weaknesses of different varieties of wood.

makes the point that even rural Americans were familiar with powered machinery to grind their grain, cut their wood, and card their wool. The tool chest of James Locke, New York cabinetmaker, speaks eloquently of the urban craftsman's skills.

Americans' familiarity with machines made it easy for them to embrace the technology of the British Industrial Revolution. The railroad, the factory, and the steam engine soon found wide acceptance in Amer-

The tools of an early 19th-century cabinetmaker, James Locke.

ica. Samuel Slater, apprentice to a British textile mill manager, came in 1790 to Pawtucket, Rhode Island, where, with backing from an American merchant and the assistance of American mechanics, he established the first successful American spinning mill. A spinning machine from that mill is on display.

The locomotive *John Bull,* the oldest operable self-propelled vehicle in the world, is another example of a technology transfer. The president of the Camden and Amboy Railroad of New Jersey purchased the locomotive in England and had it shipped across the Atlantic in 1831. It is displayed here as it crossed the first American iron railroad bridge. A film shows the *John Bull* in operation in 1981.

Federal, state, and local governments encouraged the development of industry through economic policies—tariffs, taxes, and direct investment. The patent system too promoted

invention and innovation. On display are models of some of the most well-known inventions of the period, including Eli Whitney's cotton gin, Elias Howe's sewing machine, and the telegraph of Samuel F. B. Morse.

Among 10 case studies investigating examples of early American industry are the Oliver Evans automated gristmill (one of the earliest examples of automation) and the Tredegar Iron Works, of Richmond, Virginia, where slave labor produced iron for much of the South.

The work of the machinist was of critical importance to the Industrial Revolution, and the machine shop of Augustus Alfred of Harwinton, Connecticut, is re-created as it might have looked about 1855. An interactive videodisk program allows visitors to see the machines in operation.

Production machinery is highlighted in three sections. John Howe's 1840 pin-making machine—one of the oldest surviving pieces of automated machinery—stands behind a video of the machine in operation. Many Americans were first introduced to factory labor in textile mills; the famous Lowell mill girls are featured in a re-created factory setting with two of the earliest surviving factory spinning frames. The arms industry saw the most extensive development of mechanized industrialized production. At armories in Springfield, Massachusetts, and Harpers Ferry, Virginia (now West Virginia), special machinery, interchangeable parts, and a complex system of management and control were used in making guns.

The final section of *Engines of Change* takes stock of the Industrial Revolution in 1860. Here are displayed dozens of manufactured objects of the day; here also is shown, in graphics and words, the nature of the new American working class and something of the costs of America's

The Industrial Revolution brought forth previously unimaginable numbers and varieties of goods for American consumers.

industrial development. A short video epilogue outlines the future course of the Industrial Revolution and sets the scene for a visit to the rest of the Museum's exhibitions about technology and industry.

Hall of Agriculture

The tools, machines, and vehicles in this hall are three-dimensional evidence of a profound change in rural America over the last century and a half. At the entrance stands a mighty International Harvester tractor Model 1486, built in 1979. This giant has a 156-horsepower engine, power steering and brakes, an AM-FM radio and cassette deck, even air conditioning. Beside it is "Old Red," built in 1943, the first commercial spindle cotton picker and a machine that helped to end the age of hand-picking in the South. Just across the aisle is a Huber steam tractor of 1924. A workhorse in its day, the Huber delivered 18 horsepower, rumbled along at two miles per hour, and burned roughly two pounds of coal a minute.

These three machines represent the culmination of a story told from its beginnings in the rest of the hall, where the pieces of agricultural history are on display—from hand tools to horse-drawn tools to the machines that ended much of the horse's labor on the farm. Clearly shown is the progression from manpower to horsepower to steam power to the power of the internal combustion engine.

A 1740 plow from Ipswich, Massachusetts, hangs beside a panel

Part of the gearing of a 19th-century mule-powered cotton gin, in place in Forsyth, Georgia, before it was dismantled and brought to the Museum.

The 156-horsepower International Harvester tractor Model 1486 was driven to Washington, D.C., as part of a demonstration by the American Agricultural Movement in 1979 and later donated to the Museum.

The 1918 Waterloo Boy, which ran on kerosene, was one of the most widely used tractors of its day.

A 1924 John Deere Model D tractor.

describing Thomas Jefferson's "scientific" design for a wooden moldboard plow. Beneath them stretches a platform of plows, including a wheeled plow of 1769 and a full-scale reproduction of the steel plow John Deere introduced in 1837. The cleaner cut of the high-quality steel blade of Deere's plow increased roughly tenfold the number of acres a farmer could turn in a season and helped make Deere's name revered in American agriculture.

Throughout the hall, graphics, hand tools, and horse-drawn implements of the 18th and 19th centuries illustrate the stages of bringing forth a harvest, from seed to crop to seed again. A 19th-century scythe hangs near two hoes and a wooden hayfork. Horse-drawn equipment such as a cultivator, a roller, a harrow, and planters line two walls. Beyond them is a McCormick Self-Rake Reaper of 1895, a descendant of the machine that revolutionized harvesting and made Cyrus McCormick a millionaire in the mid-19th century. Beyond the reaper is a hand-cranked winnowing machine to separate wheat from chaff, and between them stands a contraption that powered threshers and other farm machinery for decades before the rise of steam power—a horse-powered treadmill.

A huge combined harvester-thresher, an early version of the modern combine, stands at the center of the hall. This combine was built in California in 1886 by Benjamin Holt, who would later found the Caterpillar Tractor Company. Although they caught on slowly at first, combines incorporated an irresistible idea—one machine that could reap, thresh, separate, and winnow grain in the field.

The steam engine and the internal-combustion engine eventually supplanted horses both to move and to power machines. In one corner of the hall stands a red and black 1869 portable steam engine made by the J. I. Case company, the first such engine the firm produced. Early internal-combustion tractors on display include the 1918 Waterloo Boy and the Hart-Parr tractor of 1903. Both ran on kerosene. Next to gearing from a 19th-century cotton gin from Forsyth, Georgia, sits a shiny green and yellow 1924 John Deere tractor Model D, the machine that launched Deere into the tractor market.

The Hall of American Maritime Enterprise

The United States, like many countries, grew up around seaports. Even today all but four of the nation's 20 largest cities have major harbors. Lining the walls of the first gallery in this hall are images of harbors and models of the kinds of ships that have kept harbors alive for centuries, such as steam tugs and pilot schooners. In the next gallery looms the oldest marine propeller known to survive. It pushed and ultimately sank the ship *Indiana* when in 1858 one of its blades broke off, punctured the hull, and

The oldest commercial marine propeller known to have survived, from the Indiana, *a ship which sank in Lake Superior in 1858.*

The engine of the Indiana *comes to rest beside its massive boiler on the deck of the U.S. Army Corps of Engineers' derrick barge the* Coleman.

sent the vessel to the bottom of Lake Superior. Some 18 tons of the *Indiana's* remains were recovered in 1979.

Ship models in the next room show the evolution of the sailing vessels from ships not much larger than the *Mayflower* to huge coastal cargo schooners like the *C. C. Mengel, Jr.* of 1916. Chinese ceramics, a tea chest, an Oriental porcelain figurine, and more ship models help tell the story of the China trade and the clipper ship. Just beyond the clippers, a whaling song's lament drifts out from an alcove. There rests a whaleboat from the *Charles W. Morgan*, filled with harpoons, lances, buckets, kegs, and rope.

With the Louisiana Purchase of 1803 and the opening of the Great Lakes, the United States had thousands of miles of inland waterways to explore, travel, and put to use. The steam engine enabled Americans to over-come the relentless currents of the country's rivers. The inventions of American steamboat pioneers, as well as their public squabbles over patents and monopolies, are described here. A patent granted to John Fitch by Louis XVI of France in 1791 hangs above the oldest surviving steam plant built in America, the engine and boiler of John Stevens's *Little Juliana.*

Next are models of the long, white "wedding cake" steamboats that plied the Ohio, Missouri, and Mississippi rivers. Exhibits on snags, ice, and other perils of the inland waterways lead to the story of commerce on the Great Lakes, America's inland seas. A 1970s pilot house of a towboat, complete with sonar, radar, and other modern navigational equipment, brings the story up-to-date.

As steamships and sailing vessels grew faster through the 19th century, ocean travel boomed and disasters

A whaleboat from the Charles W. Morgan.

A Francis Metallic Life Car of 1850 hangs just beyond a huge black bell buoy used in the Chesapeake Bay.

A gallery devoted to the seaman shows a tattoo parlor and several examples of scrimshaw, the art of carving the teeth or bones of whales.

followed apace. A huge Fresnel lighthouse lens of 1872 and a Francis Metallic Life Car of 1850 represent a few of the steps taken to guard lives at sea. Life jackets from the *Titanic* and the *Morro Castle* and newspaper articles of the period recall these famous disasters in the Atlantic.

The merchant ships and luxury liners of the 20th century fill most of the rest of the hall. Descriptions of the growth of the U.S. Merchant Marine during World War I lead to models of a World War II Liberty ship of 1941–45 and a Victory ship of 1944–45. Modern commercial shipping is represented in models of freighters from 1919 to 1971. Down a stairway and through catwalks sits the huge gray 750-horsepower steam engine of the 1920 U.S. Coast Guard buoy tender *Oak*. The engine gave the vessel steadfast service until 1971.

A gallery entitled "The Only Way to Cross" describes the passenger service across the Atlantic from 1818 on. A table setting, champagne bucket, and other artifacts capture the elegance of the SS *United States*, the finest vessel of its kind. A small gallery at the end of the hall is devoted to the seaman, his work, and his arts, especially tattooing and scrimshaw, the art of carving the teeth or bones of whales.

Hall of Road Transportation
For most of the nation's history, the power that pulled wagons and carriages had hooves. The oldest vehicle on display in the hall is a two-wheeled, two-passenger chaise of 1770 from New England. A four-wheeled coachee of 1810, also on display, held six passengers and a driver and was a popular conveyance in cities and for traveling.

Outshining its neighbors is a bright yellow Concord coach of 1848, a small stagecoach. Concord coaches traveled the roads of the United States, Australia, South Africa, and South America from the late 1820s through the days of early motor vehicles. Pianobox buggies like the dour black model on display were mass-produced from the 1870s on and were among the most popular American horse-drawn vehicles until the 1920s.

Beside these carriages stand a dozen or so examples of a vehicle that helped to end their days—the bicycle. Production of bicycles in America rose from roughly 200,000 in 1889 to 1,000,000 in 1899. Bicycles on display range from an 1818 European forerunner of the modern bicycle, called a draisine, to a 1989 Stumpjumper. A velocipede of 1869 stands near two high-wheelers, or "ordinaries," one an uncommon child's ordinary of about 1885 and the other a Columbian ordinary of 1888.

The oldest self-propelled road vehicle in the Museum's collections is a steam-powered carriage built in 1866 by Richard Dudgeon of New York City. Around the corner is Sylvester Roper's 1869 steam bicycle and its distant descendant, a 1914 Pope motorcycle.

This gasoline carriage, designed by Elwood Haynes and built in 1894, cruised along at about seven miles per hour.

This red velocipede of 1869 represents a typical early example of pedal power.

Richard Petty drove this 1984 Pontiac stock car to his 200th victory on the Grand National Stock Car Circuit.

This Yamaha SR185 motorcycle, modified by the Rifle Fairing Company in 1982, set a record by traveling 372 miles on one gallon of gasoline.

The automobile and the 20th century roared in together. The hall presents vehicles driven by both steam and internal combustion, including a 1903 Oldsmobile Curved Dash Runabout, which sold for $650; some 4,000 were sold in 1903, more than any other gasoline automobile. A 1903 Winton touring car displayed here was the first automobile to cross the United States, a trip taking 63 days in that year. The 1913 Model T Ford was cheap and durable enough for rural roads and chores around the farm. It was the most popular car in the country between 1909 and 1927.

Technological advances in automobiles brought, among other things, greater speed. The hall captures the engineering, art, and excitement of high-speed automobile racing in the fiery red 1968 STP-Brawner Hawk in which Mario Andretti won the 1969 Indianapolis 500 and the 1984 Pontiac stock car that Richard Petty drove to his unequalled two hundredth victory on the Grand National Stock Car circuit.

Parking meters, travel literature, highway signs, and gas pumps are just a few of the other travel accessories on display. Beneath the vehicles are examples of the kinds of road surfaces they might have rolled along: granite blocks, wooden planks, cobblestones, and others.

Railroad Hall

The rise of the railroad revolutionized travel and commerce in 19th-century America. At mid-century, most people and freight still traveled by water, on a horse, or in wagons and carriages. In 1830 there were only 23 miles of railroad track in the country. But by the end of the Civil War, America had 35,000 miles of track;

The Pioneer *was built by Seth Wilmarth of Boston in 1851. In 1862 Confederate cavalry general J. E. B. Stuart and his troopers damaged the locomotive when they burned the Chambersburg, Pennsylvania, railroad yard.*

*The 1401, a PS-4 Pacific-type locomotive built in 1926, is the giant of
the Railroad Hall; it stretches 92 feet long and weighs 561,600 pounds.*

The Phantom *was completed in 1857 by William Mason of Taunton, Massachusetts, for the Toledo and Illinois Railroad. This model recaptures Mason's eye for beauty and attention to detail.*

by 1883, 93,000 miles; and, by 1900, 186,000 miles. Near the entrance of the hall is an iron, silver, and gold spike that symbolizes the unification of the country by rail. It was used in the ceremonies at Promontory, Utah, on May 10, 1869, marking the opening of the transcontinental railroad.

The prime mover behind this revolution was the steam locomotive. One black cylinder, the boiler, and a few other parts are all that remain of the *Stourbridge Lion*, 1829, the first steam

locomotive to operate in the Western Hemisphere. But a model nearby shows off the engine in its original gaudy yellow and black livery.

The *Pioneer* ran on the Cumberland Valley Railroad in the 1850s. Confederate cavalry officer J. E. B. Stuart and his troopers damaged the engine when they burned the Chambersburg, Pennsylvania, railroad yard. Repaired, the locomotive ran regularly until 1880 and occasionally until a decade later.

The electric streetcar, number 303, carried passengers from the wharves on the Potomac to the northern boundaries of the nation's capital at the turn of the century.

The John Bull *is the oldest operable locomotive in the world. It was built in England in 1831 for service on the Camden and Amboy Railroad of New Jersey, one of the first public railroads in the United States.*

Looming over the *Pioneer* is the Museum's colossus, the green-and-black Southern Railway *1401*. Built in 1926, the *1401* weighs 561,600 pounds (engine and tender), stretches almost 92 feet in length, delivers 45,000 pounds of pulling power, and hauled passengers some two million miles from 1926 to 1951. An audiotape re-creates the sounds of the *1401* chugging out of a station, and panels reveal how the locomotive was pulled through the streets of Washington and deposited in the hall in November 1961, more than two years before the Museum opened.

Along one wall, a series of finely executed models presents the history of locomotives. These include the first steam locomotive, Englishman Rich-ard Trevithick's 1804 machine built to carry iron on a tram road; English builder Robert Stephenson's 1829 *Rocket*, the first engine to combine the essential elements of the modern steam locomotive; and some two dozen other miniature prime movers all the way up to the Union Pacific's *4000*, a giant articulated engine of the 1940s.

A diesel engine of 1934 towers over a model of the train it pulled, the stainless steel *Pioneer Zephyr*, and leads to several more models of electric railway trains and diesel locomotives. Diesel electric locomotives pushed most of the steam engines off the rails in the late 1940s.

Locomotives, of course, are not the whole story of travel on rails. Models show the evolution of the freight and passenger car and the streetcar through the 19th century. An 1836 passenger coach, a cable car used on the Seattle City Railway from 1888 to about 1910, and an electric streetcar that ran in Washington, D.C., at the turn of the century are on display. The *Olomana* labored in the fields of a Hawaiian sugar plantation for 62 years. This little engine was the product of the world's largest manufacturer of locomotives, the Baldwin Locomotive Works of Philadelphia, and represents many other machines of its stature used at lumberyards and construction sites from 1870 to about 1910. The *John Bull,* the oldest complete locomotive in the collection and one of the earliest preserved railway engines in the world, is exhibited near the entrance to the *Engines of Change* exhibition.

Civil Engineering: Hall of Bridges and Tunnels

At one exit from the Railroad Hall are three timber arches, which explain in three-dimensional form the techniques of supporting earth while the permanent masonry lining of a tunnel is laid. A single cast-iron ring is a one-third scale model of the support lining New York City's Lincoln Tunnel.

Dioramas line the right wall of this tunnel on tunneling. A model shows the first tunnel ever constructed underwater—beneath the River Thames in London between 1825 and 1842. Other models represent the construction of the St. Clair River Tunnel, which in 1890 connected the railway systems of Canada and the United States and was the first tunnel under a North American river. Artifacts, dioramas, models, and illustrations also describe the evolution of tunneling in solid rock.

Numbered cases in the hall describe by images, models, and artifacts the materials and techniques of bridge building from Roman times to the present. The Romans were masters of the stone bridge as they were the perfecters of the arch. Models show the Pont du Gard—an aqueduct near Nimes, France—built by the Romans between 27 B.C. and A.D. 14, and the bridge over the River Tagus in Spain, built from A.D. 98 to 105 and still used today.

Huge timbers hanging high on the walls and models help to illustrate the way early truss bridges were built. Other models show the first major suspension bridge, completed in 1826 over the Menai Straits in Wales by English engineer Thomas Telford, and the world's first cast-iron bridge, built over the River Severn at Coalbrookdale, England, in 1779.

In the mid-19th century, the rise of the railroads put new demands on bridge builders here and abroad. In 1850 English engineer Robert Stephenson built a railroad bridge over the Menai Straits—not far from Telford's highway bridge—that featured two huge wrought-iron tubular girders through which the trains passed. The 19th century's master of

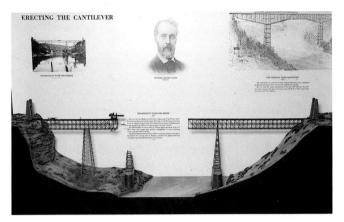

ERECTING THE CANTILEVER

This display on the cantilever bridge is one of dozens explaining bridge building. The bridge is shown under construction, emphasizing the principle of the cantilever.

the suspension bridge, John Augustus Roebling, proved the strength and practicality of iron-wire suspension bridges with his 821-foot span over the Niagara River. Completed in 1855, it was the world's only major railroad suspension bridge. A section of the original cable is shown with a model of the bridge.

The Brooklyn Bridge, designed by Roebling and completed under the direction of his son Washington in 1883, was the world's first large steel-wire suspension bridge. Several models, diagrams, and photographs describe and illustrate in detail the construction of its massive stone piers and steel cables. Photographs show other modern steel bridges, such as the Henry Hudson Bridge, the Mack-

inac Bridge, and the Firth of Forth Bridge built near Edinburgh, Scotland, in 1890.

Reinforced concrete has come to play a vital role in bridge building in modern times because of its adaptability, great strength, and comparatively low cost. Models show the designs of many plain-concrete and reinforced-concrete bridges, such as the Prospect Park Bridge, completed in 1871 in Brooklyn, New York, and the elegant Liège Exposition Bridge of 1905, designed by French engineer François Hennebique, a pioneer in the use of reinforced concrete. A photograph also shows one of the world's longest concrete arches, the Sando Bridge, which spans the Angerman River in Sweden.

Hall of Power Machinery

Here visitors will find the history of power and machinery tangible on all sides in pumps, boilers, turbines, waterwheels, and engines. Some of this machinery comes to life in regular demonstrations (ask at the information desks for days and times). In models and machines, this hall follows the development of increasingly efficient power machinery to show a nation, even a world, abuilding.

Several exhibits on waterwheels and water turbines remind us that for millennia people have relied on the power of falling water. Artifacts displayed include a Francis reaction turbine of about 1880, typifying the most efficient later water turbines, and a huge red Riedler pumping engine of 1901 driven by a Pelton impulse turbine.

The steam engine was a device of liberation. It freed mankind from complete dependence on primary sources of power: wind, water, and human and animal muscle power. Englishman Thomas Savery designed the first commercially useful steam engine in 1712; his creation was put to work pumping water from mines, the most important early application of steam power. A model of his invention appears here.

Another Englishman, James Watt, later introduced several significant innovations: the separate condenser, which alone increased the efficiency of the steam engine fourfold; the governor, which automatically controls the speed of an engine under varying loads; the double-acting steam engine, which used the direct power of expanding steam to drive a piston back and forth; and the linkages that made possible the conversion of a steam engine's reciprocating motion into rotary motion to drive machinery.

The cylinder of a Naylor-Corliss mill engine of 1885. George Corliss's improved valve gear gave this engine a dramatic increase in efficiency.

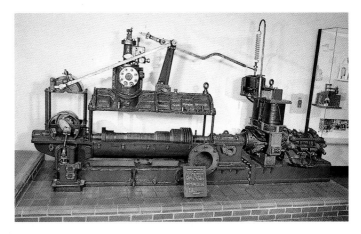

A 1905 turbogenerator of the English engineer Charles Parsons, pioneer designer of the commercially successful steam turbine.

The Curtis-General Electric steam turbine of 1927 is cut away to reveal its blading.

With these last two innovations, the steam engine became the power behind the Industrial Revolution. A large model of a Watt engine of 1788 shows the workings of a double-acting mill engine.

Richard Trevithick of England and Oliver Evans of the United States independently pioneered the use of steam at higher pressures to do more work and use less fuel. Models of their high-pressure steam engines, both built in the first decade of the 19th century, are displayed here. Nearby stand the oldest surviving relics of an American-built stationary steam engine, a Holloway 10-horsepower engine of 1819.

Among the steam engines on display are a bright yellow Naylor-Corliss mill engine of 1885 and a black Porter-Allen engine of 1881, the earliest high-speed steam engine. A Skinner engine of 1926 incorporates the final major improvement in steam-engine design, the uniflow principle, perfected by the German engineer Johann Stumpf, and its highly efficient valves, porting, and piston.

The steam-driven Frick ammonia compressor, this one from 1898, was a standard of the refrigeration industry from 1880 to 1920. Some Frick compressors of the period are still at work today.

Traditional steam engines gave way to the more efficient steam turbine, in which steam striking a series of radial blades produced a high-speed rotary motion ideal for driving electric generators. Included here are two early turbogenerators of the English engineer Charles Parsons, pioneer designer of the commercially successful steam turbine, and a Curtis-General Electric steam turbine of 1927, cut away to reveal its blading.

Like the steam engine, the internal-combustion engine has a long and venerable history. In 1799 the French chemist and engineer Philippe Lebon patented a design for an internal-combustion engine that included the compression of combustion gases, electric ignition, and a gas generator, all elements that foreshadowed the modern engine. Models show several early internal-combustion engines, including the first commercially practical internal-combustion design, built in France in 1860 by J. J. Étienne Lenoir. Some of his engines remained in use until 1910.

The father of the modern internal-combustion engine was the German engineer Nikolaus August Otto. With his partner, Eugen Langen, Otto introduced his first gas engine at the Paris Exposition of 1867. Its fuel economy made it a rapid commercial success. A watershed was Otto's four-stroke engine of 1876, an engine of greatly improved performance and the forerunner of the modern gasoline engine. Engines of both types are exhibited, occasionally in operation.

In 1892 another German engineer, Rudolf Diesel, patented an engine that relied on the temperature of ultrahigh compression of air inside a cylinder to ignite fuel without flame or spark ignition. Most early diesels were stationary engines. Here a section of a three-cylinder engine of 1905, the American Diesel, stands near a General Motors diesel of a type still used today to drive generators and other machinery as well as vehicles and boats.

The final section of the hall traces the history of refrigeration from ancient times to modern and touches on both the commercial use of natural ice as a cooling agent and the work of early experimenters in producing cold by a variety of chemical and physical methods. Mechanical refrigeration is represented by several recent machines on display, including a Frick steam-powered ammonia compressor of 1898, a standard of the industry from 1880 to 1920, and a Carrier four-stage centrifugal compressor of 1922, a type used widely in modern large-scale commercial air conditioning.

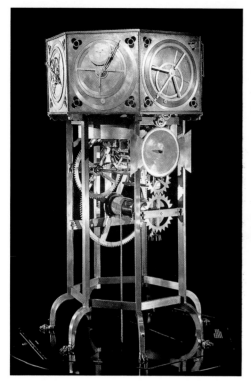

Giovanni de'Dondi of Padua, Italy, built his astronomical clock in about 1350. This reproduction is based on descriptions in manuscripts of the period.

The Great Historical Clock of America, almost 13 feet tall, was built by an unknown craftsman in about 1893.

Hall of Timekeeping and Light Machinery

From sundials on, what most devices in this hall reveal is the fundamental requirement for measuring time— some steady process, like the burning of a candle, or a regular, recurring event such as the passage of the sun overhead or the vibration of an atom. Visitors can see sundials, water clocks, and sandglasses from ancient Egyptian times to the 18th century.

Mechanical clocks appeared in the late 13th century. A reconstruction of the clock of Giovanni de'Dondi of Padua, Italy, stands at the entrance to the hall. One of the most complex early timekeepers, it was built in about 1350 and is reproduced here from manuscripts of the period. In the early 16th century, probably in Italy, the substitution of a spring for a weight to drive a clock, and refinements to the spring itself, made possible smaller timepieces, even early watches. Elegant, intricate small clocks and watches of the 16th and 17th centuries are on display.

Dutch astronomer Christian Huygens radically improved the accuracy of timepieces with his invention in 1656 of a clock regulated by a pendulum. A clock from 17th-century Turin, Italy, and Dutch, English, and German examples from the 17th and 18th centuries feature pendulums. A

Acorn clocks are named for the whimsical, graceful shape of their cases. The Forestville Manufacturing Company of Bristol, Connecticut, produced this clock in about 1849.

This marine chronometer of 1812 is shown in a period room that contains some of the tools of its maker, William Bond of Boston. Such portable chronometers were indispensable for determining longitude at sea.

central section shows the workings of huge tower clocks. A re-creation of the shop of William Bond and Son, one of the most important 19th-century American makers of scientific instruments and precision timekeepers, displays tools of the trade.

Along one wall some two dozen shelf clocks trace the development of American wooden-works clocks and brass clocks and the contributions of important clock makers such as Seth Thomas and John Ives. These clocks lead to an alcove housing magnificent tall case clocks, such as the 1770 creation of the American scientist David Rittenhouse.

On a platform leading from the hall stand precision clocks called regulators, such as the 1855–59 clock of E. Howard and Company of Boston. Regulators were used to set or control other clocks and to mark the exact time of astronomical observations. Atomic clocks, which measure time by the constant frequency of radiation emitted from atoms, replaced quartz crystal timekeepers in the 1950s as the final arbiters of accuracy. A quartz clock of 1929 and a modern atomic clock indicator stand side by side. Six hundred years ago, clocks commonly varied 15 minutes a day; atomic clocks vary only about one-millionth of a second a year.

Locks, hinges, keys, reproductions,

"The Electric Kiss," an 18th-century parlor game, is reenacted in the Hall of Electricity.

and illustrations, including a lock plate excavated from the ruins of Pompeii, show the history of locks from ancient Egyptian times to the 20th century. Another row of cases holds a collection of early phonographs, including one of the first machines of Thomas Edison to record and reproduce sound. A Victor Talking Machine of 1903 bears perhaps the most famous trademark in American business, a dog turning its ear attentively to a phonograph beneath the words "His Master's Voice." A Victor Model XI on display, called a Victrola, was the most popular machine from about 1911 to 1925.

Directly across from the phonographs is a long row of typewriters. An Englishman, Henry Mills, was awarded a patent in England for a typewriter in 1714, and American inventor William Burt won a patent for his typographer in 1829. But the first practical typewriter was patented by a trio of American inventors, Carlos Glidden, Samuel W. Soule, and Christopher Sholes. Sholes sold the rights to the invention to the Remington company in 1873 for $12,000—and the typewriter industry was born.

Hall of Electricity

A small introductory gallery shows 18th- and 19th-century electrostatic apparatus, including a globe machine probably designed by Benjamin Franklin, several Leyden jars for storing electric charges, and a twin-plate generator of about 1800 in an active

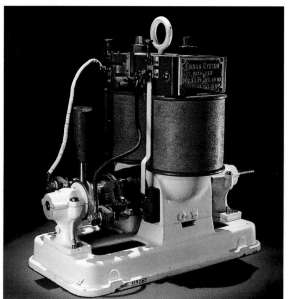

An Edison electric motor of about 1890.

A late 19th-century ammeter.

tableau of a parlor game called the "electric kiss."

Lighting a Revolution At the end of the 19th century, a new way of transmitting power came to the fore—electricity. In 1876, at the Philadelphia Centennial Exhibition, a few arc lights were shown. They were very bright, suitable only for large open spaces. Three years later, Thomas Edison announced his invention of the incandescent light bulb, and on New Year's Eve in 1879 he drew a crowd of 3,000 visitors to his Menlo Park, New Jersey, complex to see the buildings and grounds aglow in the softer light of his creation. *Lighting a Revolution* explains in detail that Edison's revolution was no overnight affair.

The first section of the exhibition displays and describes 19th-century batteries, motors, generators, meters, magnets, arc lamps, and even tentative incandescent lamps that formed a technical base for Edison's work. The next section looks more closely at Edi-

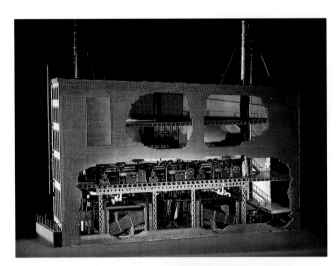

A model of Thomas Edison's Pearl Street Station in New York City, which began generating electricity on September 4, 1882.

Steam power and electric power meet in this display of a Porter-Allen steam engine of 1888 (foreground) driving an Edison electric generator.

son and his laboratory through photographs of him, his family, and his colleagues; samples of the materials he tested in his search for a workable filament; some of his tools; and several of his early light bulbs. Edison and his colleagues produced not merely a light bulb, but an electrical system, and the next section tells the story of his early power plants, including the first central station at Pearl Street in New York City, which began producing power on September 4, 1882.

Edison's success drew competitors, some of whom improved on his methods, especially through the introduction of alternating current, which ultimately supplanted his direct-current system. The next section of the exhibition shows the lamps, meters, generators, and other devices of some of these competitors and explains the reasons why alternating current proved superior to direct current.

In 1895 a large remote generating station began producing electricity at Niagara Falls. Less than two decades after Edison's invention, electricity thus was accepted as a principal means of power transmission. A revolution had taken place. Cheap electric power made new industrial processes possible, such as the economical production of aluminum. Eventually this power reached the city and the home, where its influence is made clear in a case filled with early 20th-century appliances such as fans, coffee pots, and vacuum cleaners.

Hall of Physical Sciences

In the entrance to the Hall of Physical Sciences, concerned largely with American scientific discovery of the 19th and 20th centuries, is a case describing the evolution of American surveying instruments. Artifacts include British and American compasses, surveying chains, theodolites, and transits from the late 18th century. Another display explores the work of physicist Albert Abraham Michelson, in 1907 the first American to win a Nobel prize.

Re-creations of two chemistry laboratories stand along one wall of the hall. The first represents the late 18th-century lab of Joseph Priestley, who isolated and described oxygen, chlorine, and other elements. The lab displays some of his apparatus, including a static electric machine, a gas-generating apparatus, and a huge magnifying glass called a burning lens. Next to Priestley's laboratory is another modeled after that of chemist Ira Remsen, the discoverer of saccharin. His equipment includes electrochemical batteries, a precision balance, crucibles, and retorts.

A section on meteorology begins with the invention of the barometer in 1643 by the Italian mathematician and physicist Evangelista Torricelli, a student of Galileo's. Artifacts, replicas, and illustrations in this section describe several early meteorologists and devices of the 17th century. The next display examines the role of the first Secretary of the Smithsonian, Joseph Henry, in the development of

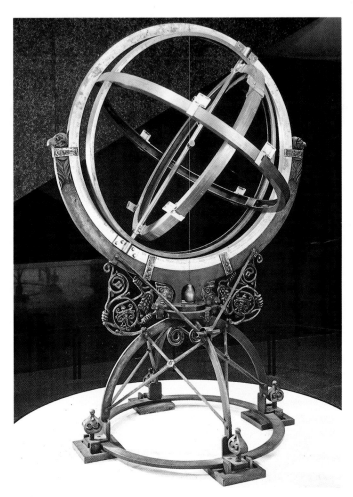

This modern reproduction of an equatorial armillary was built according to the specifications of the 16th-century Dutch astronomer Tycho Brahe.

This re-creation of the late 18th-century laboratory of chemist Joseph Priestley contains some of the glassware he used in his Northumberland, Pennsylvania, laboratory.

a system of centralized meteorological observations in the United States, work that led to the formation of the U.S. Weather Service.

By the early 19th century experimenters were taking meteorological readings in balloons or from instruments sent aloft on kites. The combination of equipment that records and transmits this kind of information is called a radiosonde. Several late 19th- and early 20th-century radiosondes are displayed here. A modern descendant of these instruments, a rocket-sonde, propels equipment aloft to altitudes of 80,000 to 300,000 feet.

The rest of the hall is devoted mainly to astronomy. Two cases describe the work of three important 19th-century American astronomers, John W. Draper, his son Henry, and Lewis Morris Rutherfurd. Among the objects on display are Henry Draper's daguerreotypes of the sun and moon from about 1860 and Rutherfurd's 1868 and 1879 photographs of a star and the sun.

Just beyond the work of the Drapers and Rutherfurd stand the kinds of instruments they might have used, the main ingredients of a 19th-century observatory: an equatorial telescope, a chronograph, an observatory clock, and a meridian circle, a device used to detect the precise moment that a heavenly body passes overhead. Artifacts and illustrations nearby show the evolution of telescope lenses, from a 9 ½-inch lens used at the U.S. Naval Observatory in 1845 to the 200-inch giant installed on Mt. Palomar in California in 1948. In addition, there are a 24-inch reflecting telescope from Yerkes Observatory

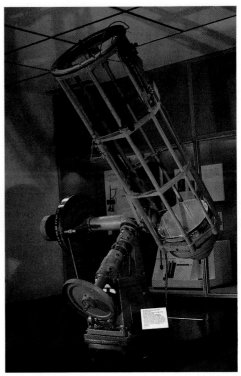

John Peate, a retired minister and amateur astronomer, made this 62-inch telescope mirror in 1898. At the time it was by far the largest glass mirror ever made in the United States.

A 24-inch photographic telescope designed and built by George Willis Ritchey in about 1900.

and one built by amateur telescope maker Martin Rasmussen, a Danish immigrant, in about 1931.

The last exhibit in the hall is a diorama re-creating the workshop of Henry Fitz, America's first commercial telescope maker. Using the tools shown here, Fitz created more than 50 astronomical telescopes. His well-made, moderately priced telescopes helped popularize astronomy in the United States.

Hall of the History of Medicine

This hall begins, as medicine did, with a mixture of practical observations and religion. At the entrance are several unusual artifacts that speak to people's faith in faith as a cure for

A period setting showing the office of Dr. Charles E. Kells in about 1905. Kells was the first dentist to use X rays.

The core of an automated, computerized, transverse axial (ACTA) scanner stands in front of cabinets containing the computer, televisions, and other control units that help form its images. This machine was the first whole-body CAT scanner.

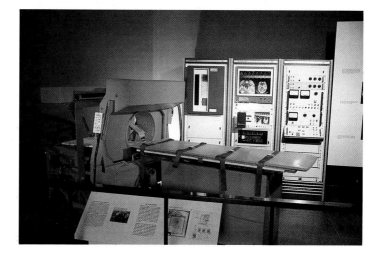

injury and disease, including a 17th-century touchpiece thought to cure epilepsy, then called the "king's evil." Nearby are 19th- and 20th-century examples of quackery, such as a static machine of 1895, which stands ready to administer an electric "spray" or "breeze" to a patient to cure nervous or muscular disorders.

The work of early microscopists is also taken up at the beginning of the hall. The English scientist Robert Hooke observed cork cells under a microscope in 1665. A replica of one of his early microscopes is on display, as is one of Anton van Leeuwenhoek, a Dutch naturalist, who became the first person to see bacteria. Several examples from across Europe illustrate the improvements in microscopes that gradually made them indispensable in medicine.

A re-creation of a bacteriological laboratory of about 1905 shows instruments used by Simon Flexner, the first director of the Rockefeller Institute of Medicine in New York City, and Frederick Novy, a pioneering American microbiologist.

Scarificators, lancets, and an elegant sky-blue ceramic jar bearing the label "leeches" introduce the history of bloodletting in the next exhibit. Two nearby cases delve into methods of seeing inside the body and hearing its sounds. They contain stethoscopes, tongue depressors, speculums, and 20th-century otoscopes, bronchoscopes, and laryngoscopes. The eyes have displays of their own, which include the history of spectacles and the evolution of the tools of ophthalmology. Anyone who wears glasses will recognize the modern ophthalmoscopes here.

Techniques for probing the body fill several cases and platforms in this area. Wall cases and a diorama describe the discovery of X rays by German physician Wilhelm Roentgen in 1895 and the early use of X rays in America. A small case holds one of the X-ray tubes Roentgen used in his early experiments. Across from it stands a period room with the X-ray equipment of Dr. C. Edmund Kells, the first dentist to use X rays to diagnose tooth disease. A large exhibit, "Body Imaging," presents the prototypes of three modern diagnostic devices: an ultrasound machine, a computerized axial tomography (CAT) scanner, and a nuclear magnetic resonance (NMR) imager. Each in its own way creates an image of the interior of the body, sometimes a portrait of astounding clarity. Labels describe the development, operation, and uses of the machines.

Medicine is as much concerned with healing as with discovery and diagnosis. Exhibits in this hall deal with nursing, surgery, dentistry, and pharmacy. A tableau shows Linda Richards, "America's first trained nurse," administering to a patient at Boston's Massachusetts General Hospital. Artifacts in rows of cases describing early surgery include replicas of Roman surgical instruments, 16th-century trephining instruments for surgery on the skull, and an 18th-

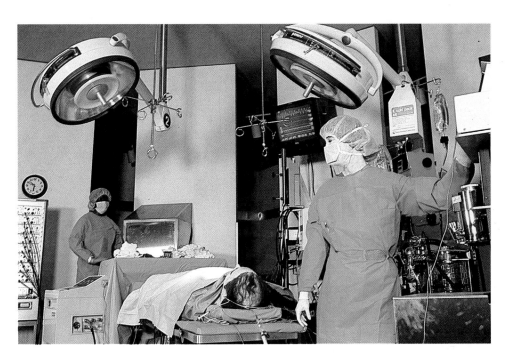

A re-creation of a modern operating room.

This re-creation of the study-workshop of an 18th-century apothecary shop shows the kinds of instruments and glassware an apothecary might have used to make drugs.

century surgical saw. Surgical instruments and equipment here include several varieties of replacement heart valves from the 1950s and 1960s; early heart bypass pumps; and a perfusion pump designed in 1935 by Nobel-prize winner Alexis Carrel and aviator Charles Lindbergh that allowed researchers to keep organs alive outside the body.

The exhibits on dentistry include arrays of dental tools; a period setting of the laboratory and study of Dr. Angle, a 19th-century American dentist who established orthodontics as a dental specialty; and a display of the dental equipment of American dentist Dr. G. V. Black, a pioneer in treating tooth decay.

The last section of the Hall of the History of Medicine (or the first, depending on how you approach the hall) explores the history of pharmacy. A re-creation of a large 18th-century European apothecary shop holds row upon row of finely decorated drug jars, some of them centuries old. In the apothecary's dispensary are mortars and pestles, balances, and, hanging from the ceiling, a crocodile, a tortoise, and other creatures. Apothecaries who claimed to derive medicines from animals sought to prove to their customers that their drugs came from genuine sources.

An American pharmacy of 1890, which once stood at Eighth and I streets in Washington, D.C., displays many artifacts both like and unlike those of its ancestor. Cosmetics and patent medicines are evident here, but elegant drug jars still line the walls, and a jar in the window testifies that the pharmacist still keeps leeches.

Surrounding the drugstores old and new are exhibits filling out the history of pharmacy. "Drugs from A to Z" (namely ambergris to zinc acetate), suggests the breadth of materials from which people have extracted ingredients with real or imagined powers of healing. Public health history is represented by a case describing the development of the public health field in New York City, includ-ing public health nursing and the early production of vaccines.

Pain and Its Relief The many methods people have used through-out history to alleviate physical suf-fering are exhibited in *Pain and Its Relief*. The exhibition addresses both the history of efforts to treat and relieve pain and the growing under-standing of the complex interactions of pain with our bodies and minds. The exhibition examines ancient tradi-tions of healing, from magic to plants, powders, and potions; surgical sleep and the introduction of inhalation anesthesia (nitrous oxide and ether) in the 1840s; the pain-relief industry since the mid-1800s and the commer-cial success of its tonics, tablets, and techniques to relieve everyday aches and pains; and 20th-century devel-opments in surgical sleep and tech-

A period setting of an American drugstore of about 1890.

niques of killing pain without loss of consciousness. A video theater featuring an introductory film, *What Is Pain?*, sets the stage for other elements of the exhibition, including early ether inhalers, the re-creation of a contemporary operating room, and even a Zander machine (used to exercise, pummel, prod, and shake out the pains of patrons at posh spas in the 1890s).

Information Age

Information Age: People, Information & Technology focuses on people more than machines and emphasizes how information technology has changed the way we live. One of the largest exhibitions ever mounted by the Smithsonian, *Information Age* draws on more than 700 objects and 700 graphics, supplemented with scores of video stations and computer-driven work stations to allow visitors hands-on use of computers and interactive equipment. Before leaving *Information Age,* visitors can print out a file of activities created on the exhibition's computer network.

The timeline of technology starts in the 1830s with the invention of the telegraph, the first means of long-distance instantaneous communication. A piece of the first transatlantic telegraph cable, which connected London with New York in 1858, is displayed. The exhibition also examines the invention of the telephone, wireless, and radio, and the ways information processing has evolved in business management, financial

A photograph of Samuel F. B. Morse rests beside his original telegraph of 1835. The paper tape in the foreground carries the first long-distance telegraph message, sent from Baltimore to Washington, D.C., in 1843.

markets, systems control, and data processing.

Specific highlights of this section include one of Samuel Morse's early telegraphs, Alexander Graham Bell's original telephone, the Hollerith tabulating system (used to compile results of the 1890 U.S. census), and vintage radio programs. A 1939 street scene allows the passerby to see how information technology that was developed over the previous century found a place in American society— in the Social Security office, a radio store, a newsstand, an office supply store, and a living room.

A five-minute film inside the Bijou Theater transports the visitor from American life in 1939 into the next section, "World War II: Mobilizing Technology," which focuses on the military uses of information technology. A full-scale re-creation of a Combat Information Center shows how electronic information from radio, radar, and sonar was plotted and analyzed. In exhibits on breaking the top-secret German ENIGMA code, visitors can encode their own names with ENIGMA, then break the code. Early experimentation with digital computers is also displayed to show the rapid wartime development of electronics. ENIAC, the largest, most powerful early computer, was built to compute ballistics tables for the Army.

Alexander Graham Bell's telephone receivers and transmitters of 1876. Bell demonstrated his invention at the Philadelphia Centennial Exhibition of 1876.

Telephones of the late 19th and early 20th centuries.

Beyond the scenes of a victory parade, a balcony overlooks a panorama of postwar possibilities. The rest of the exhibition invites comparisons between what has really occurred and the postwar projections for an atomic age with television and electronic brains. "Foundations, 1946–1960," the next section, chronicles the early development of the computer business, the transistor, high-fidelity recording, and color television.

"Into the Mainstream, 1961–1975," features computers as a part of American business life, notably in banking, airline reservations, and retail sales. The visitor sees how electrical communications became interlinked with computers and moved across such information frontiers as satellite links

*Computers are among the most conspicuous creations of the
Information Age.*

and microwave bands. The FBI's FINDER system, the first computer used for automatic fingerprint identification, provides visitors the chance to have their thumbprints read and to get a copy of the printout.

An automobile factory scene sets the stage for "Information Power, 1976–Present." Here a car body is being welded by a robot as it is being monitored by computers keeping track of everything from inventories of parts to financing. Visitors can experience the operation of a major information network as they try to produce the evening news, handle a 911 emergency, engage in international currency trading, or monitor the operations of others.

Surrounding this section is a display on the evolution of the personal computer and applications of current information technology as they emerge. Visitors can watch popular programs of the 1950s, see a re-creation of a Chicago television studio that broadcast the first televised presidential debate between John Kennedy and Richard Nixon, and participate in a poll that asks how TV has changed our culture and politics. At the end of the exhibition, the Interactive Gallery allows visitors to experiment with computer voice recognition, design a bicycle with computer-aided design, and try to run the company that produces it, as well as sample several on-line data bases, including one for the *Information Age* exhibition. (Expect interactives to change periodically to keep pace with current technologies.)

Star Wars *characters C-3PO and R2-D2 stand with a real robot used to manufacture automobiles. Courtesy Lucasfilm, Ltd.*

SECOND FLOOR

The Star-Spangled Banner

Most visitors enter the National Museum of American History through the Mall entrance, which opens onto the building's second floor. Straight ahead, a huge American flag rises high against the wall. On closer inspection, this flag turns out to be a painting of a flag. Every hour on the half hour, the towering canvas descends to reveal a larger flag behind it. This is the flag Francis Scott Key saw flying over Fort McHenry near Baltimore on the morning of September 14, 1814.

Key was detained aboard a British ship engaged in an all-night bombardment of the fort during the War of 1812. The sight of the flag inspired him to write on the back of an old letter ideas and phrases for a poem that begins with the words, "O, say can you see/By the dawn's early light. . . ." Revised and recopied when Key returned to Baltimore on September 16, the poem was delivered to a printer to be published as a handbill. Key's poem was quickly put to the tune of an old English song called "To Anacreon in Heaven."

After the War of 1812, the flag passed to the family of the fort's commander, Major George Armistead, and it was donated to the Smithsonian in 1912. The song became popular during the Civil War and, in 1931, by an act of Congress, it was officially designated the national anthem of the United States.

The Foucault Pendulum

The 240-pound brass bob of the Foucault pendulum swings across a compass design set into a hole between the first and second floors. Visitors can view the pendulum from above and below.

Using a pendulum like this in 1851, French physicist Jean Bernard Leon Foucault demonstrated the earth's rotation on its axis, the first proof of the earth's spin without reference to stars or planets. You can observe this rotation yourself either by watching the pendulum for a few minutes or by noting its position as you enter the Museum and checking back later in the day. The line of the pendulum's swing will appear to have rotated clockwise. Actually, the Museum, everyone in it, and the rest of the earth have rotated counterclockwise on the earth's axis beneath the pendulum. The free-swinging pendulum lags behind this rotation and thus seems to rotate itself.

Field to Factory: Afro-American Migration 1915–1940

Between 1915 and 1940, hundreds of thousands of black Americans left the South and migrated to the cities of the North. This "Great Migration" changed both the lives of the African-American migrants and the racial status quo in much of the North.

The movement was the result of hundreds of thousands of individual decisions to leave an old life behind in search of a brighter future. *Field to Factory* interprets the complexities

This room was both a kitchen and a gathering place for the entire family. It was part of the house of a tenant farmer in Maryland and was brought to the Museum and re-created as it might have looked early in the 20th century.

For many African Americans, the decision to move north meant leaving behind the security of family, friends, and familiar places. Migrants brought a few treasured items with them, like this sock doll in a cradle.

A re-creation of a segregated train car illustrates the conditions under which migrants traveled north.

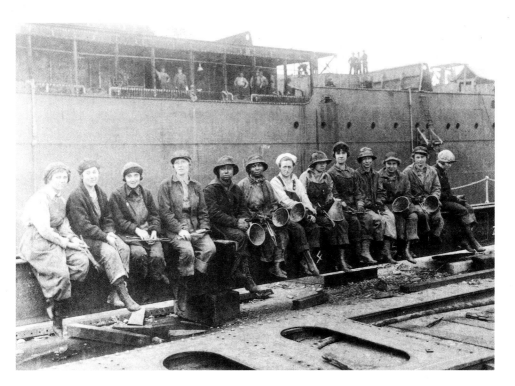

These rivet heaters and "passers on" helped build ships at the Puget Sound Navy Yard in Washington State in 1919. Industrial positions paid well compared to other jobs available to African-American women, but the work was often exhausting and monotonous, with little chance for advancement.

and effects of the Great Migration by focusing on the migrants themselves: the lives of African Americans in the South, the hopes and expectations that prompted their decision to move north, and the difficulties migrants faced in a new environment. The exhibition also examines the new technologies and culture that the migrants found in the North, the adjustments they had to make to their surroundings, and the ways the populations of Northern cities had to adjust to them.

These changes and adaptations are illustrated in several sections about life in the South, through artifacts such as a cotton gin, a school bell, signs reading "For Colored Patrons Only," and a robe and hood of the Ku Klux Klan. Other exhibits describe the life of African-American soldiers during World War I, the role of the church, and the importance of African-American newspapers such as the *Chicago Defender* in spreading news from the North. The section on life in the South ends with a Maryland tenant farmer's house, brought from eastern Maryland to the Museum and displayed as it might have looked about 1920. Its front room was both a kitchen and a gathering place for the entire family. A living history presentation at the house evokes the life of a woman staying with relatives who work the farm.

The trip north begins with a replica of the two entrances to the Ashland,

Virginia, train station—one for whites, one for blacks. Displays in this section examine the kind of industrial work and domestic work that black men and women found in the North. The importance of church and school in the North—and their differences from churches and schools in the South—are the focus of other exhibits. A re-creation of a Philadelphia row house gives an idea of the kind of homes migrants found in the North, and the kind of lives they lived in them. Chairs and other objects from a beauty salon run by Marjorie Stewart Joyner point to an African-American business community that emerged in the North. Through the more than 400 objects on display and a video presentation, *The Urban North,* the exhibition offers the opportunity to understand the significance and difficulty of the migrants' decision to leave family, home, and friends.

The Great Migration paralleled the immigration experiences of other ethnic groups who carried their hopes and dreams into an uncertain existence. *Field to Factory* gives voice to the uniqueness of the African-American experience and yet echoes the immigration experience of all peoples.

A Nation of Nations

Of all the exhibitions in the Museum, *A Nation of Nations,* in the west wing of the second floor, reaches furthest to embrace the history of the American people. A new entrance displays a photomural of street life in lower New York City about 1915, when immigrants were joining other Americans in a complex process of urbanization. Then-familiar objects of the scene include a grinder's cart, musical instruments played on the street corner, shop signs, and the humble tools of itinerant craftspeople.

Along with their crafts and meager possessions, most immigrants brought their religions to America, and here they thrived. An ark crest with the Ten Commandments in Hebrew from a Philadelphia synagogue stands beside a Protestant cross of boards—painted to read, "Get Right with God"—that once stood on a Kentucky roadside. Below rests a puppet-like figure of Jesus in His sarcophagus, from a Catholic chapel in New Mexico. Nearby, a lion mask from a Chinese Buddhist New Year's celebration floats over a Gypsy infant's vest with protective amulets.

A Nation of Nations examines the period from the late 19th century to the present by featuring the shared experiences of many American groups and individuals. It begins with Room 201 from Dunham Elementary School in Cleveland, Ohio. This classroom remained in use from 1883 to 1975 and is shown here as it might have looked about 1915. Across from the class-

An army barracks of about 1940 from Fort Belvoir, just outside Washington, D.C.

room, an American flag made entirely of red, white, and blue political campaign buttons introduces a display on American politics and labor. Here are a voting booth, ballot boxes, bumper stickers, and campaign posters from many decades past. The work of ordinary Americans is made visible in the tools they used, including a jackhammer, an axe, a sewing machine, calipers, and augers. Across the gallery is an army barracks of about 1940 from Fort Belvoir, just outside Washington, D.C. Here is a soldier's home, filled with shoes, uniforms, canteens, rifles, bunk beds, and footlockers.

Athletes and entertainers have a special place in American culture—we grant them status and celebrity as no other group of people. The areas of the exhibition devoted to these two arenas show the tools and creations

A re-creation of an Italian-American kitchen of the late 1930s, one of four rooms in an immigrant home in which objects from Italy attested to the survival of Old World traditions alongside mass-produced furniture and artifacts of 20th-century American urban life.

of the well known and lesser known. Sports equipment of anonymous amateur athletes is mixed in with Sandy Koufax's baseball glove, Chris Evert's tennis racquet, Pelé's soccer jersey, Arnold Palmer's Masters golf trophy, and Joe Louis's boxing gloves. The world of entertainment is represented by marquee posters and sheet music of all kinds, from Buffalo Bill Cody's Wild West show to minstrel shows to Broadway. Displayed in front of this backdrop of song and dance are such famous artifacts as a pair of ruby slippers worn by Judy Garland in

The Wizard of Oz, Dizzy Gillespie's trumpet, puppet Charlie McCarthy, and the chairs of Archie and Edith Bunker from the television show "All in the Family."

In the last gallery a large display case holds changing exhibits about famous Americans. In recent years these have ranged from Jimmy Durante's hat to a history of Superman from comic books to films. These icons of popular culture look out on a scene of domestic culture, an Italian-American home as it might have looked in the late 1930s.

Judy Garland, in the role of Dorothy, wore these magical ruby slippers in the American film classic The Wizard of Oz.

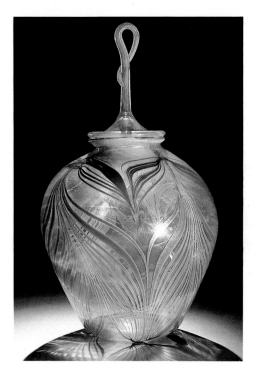

The Tiffany Glass Decorating Company founded by Louis Comfort Tiffany produced this iridescent Favrile-glass jar in the 1890s. It is one of a group that Tiffany himself selected for the Smithsonian Institution.

Ceremonial Court

Visitors to the east wing of the second floor see nearly the same sight that greeted President Theodore Roosevelt when he stepped through his own front door. The entrance to the Ceremonial Court is a re-creation of the elegant Cross Hall of the White House as it appeared after the renovation of 1902 during Roosevelt's first administration. Some of the details of the court are original. Plaster work, mantels, pilasters, giant mirrors, and crystal chandeliers came to the Smithsonian after a complete reconstruction and renovation of the White House in the early 1950s. Other architectural details were cast from the same molds that produced design elements decorating the ceilings and walls of the White House today.

Alcoves line the four sides of the court. On display are gifts to presi-

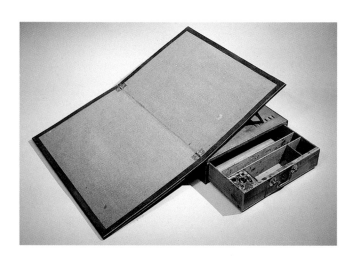

Thomas Jefferson drafted the Declaration of Independence on this portable writing desk.

This teapot, apple basket, and document box are made of tin-plated sheet iron known as tinware.

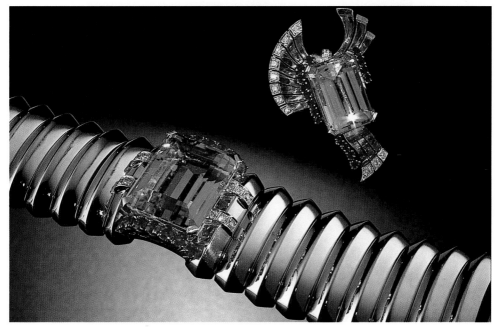

This Art Deco bracelet and brooch of 1940 are made of 14-karat gold, aquamarines, diamonds, and rubies. Yellow gold did not become fashionable for high-quality jewelry until about 1940.

Barbara Bush's blue velvet and satin gown is displayed in the
Ceremonial Court with gowns of other recent First Ladies.

dents and members of their families from foreign heads of state and other dignitaries, gowns worn by recent First Ladies, the mantel from the room in which Franklin Roosevelt delivered his fireside chats, presidential china, ceramics and glass, fine jewelry, American red earthenware, stoneware, painted tinware, glassware, silver, and White House toys—including an early teddy bear. Among the many political and presidential artifacts are the lap desk on which Thomas Jefferson wrote the Declaration of Independence, Woodrow Wilson's golf clubs, and a leather case used by George Washington for writing dispatches to the Continental Congress.

The Ceremonial Court also provides a glimpse of White House family life. A trompe l'oeil painting of two Roosevelt children, Archie and Kermit shows them at play with their pets on the grand staircase. Also on display is the White House elevator that carried the Roosevelts' pony, Algonquin, to the second-story bedroom of its master, Archie, in bed with the measles.

After the Revolution: Everyday Life in America, 1780–1800

Between the Ceremonial Court and the Star-Spangled Banner is *After the Revolution: Everyday Life in America, 1780–1800*, on the east wing of the second floor. An audiovisual program at the entrance to the hall introduces the diversity of American life in the late 18th century and some of the ordinary people that lived in the new nation. At the end of the show, the screen rises to reveal the actual log house that the Delaware farm family of Thomas and Elizabeth Springer

A room from the house of Henry Saunders, a wealthy tobacco planter in Isle of Wight County, Virginia, much as it might have looked on the day Saunders and his family moved in, about 1797.

This interior view of the log house of Thomas and Elizabeth Springer, built in New Castle County, Delaware, about 1790, shows the kinds of furniture they might have owned and used.

African traditions of basket weaving and many other crafts endured in the Americas as part of a new African-American culture.

lived in 200 years ago. Inside and outside the house, you can see the kinds of furniture, tools, and other possessions people like the Springers might have had and learn about the labors that filled their lives: cloth making, dairying, preserving, farming, and nail making.

African Americans made up about 20 percent of the population of the United States in 1790, and most of them were enslaved. The second section of the exhibition, "African-American Culture in the Chesapeake," introduces aspects of African culture, recounts the long, harrowing journey by sea, and explores the lives of African Americans in the new nation. Musical instruments, pottery, tools, and clothing are on exhibit. Other displays examine family life among African Americans, including their work, music, marriages, and burial traditions. Together the artifacts and images reveal how African culture, religion, and knowledge survived and evolved in the New World.

The "Chesapeake Planter Family" section explores the life of Henry Saunders and his family. Saunders was an ambitious planter and slaveholder in Virginia. This section features a room from the Saunders home as it might have looked on the day the family moved in and objects that illustrate social life, religion, and commerce of the period. Bills of sale and notices of slave auctions document the commercial system that kept black people enslaved. Other exhibits explain the ways slaves resisted this oppression—by fleeing north, buying their freedom, or organizing rebellions.

"The Seneca Nation of the Iroquois Confederacy" looks at the origins of the powerful Iroquois Confederacy, a league of six Indian nations bound by shared religious and cultural beliefs. Exhibits describe everyday life among the Seneca Indians through displays of a gourd rattle, a woman's over-dress, a beaded sash, corn-husk dolls, and many other objects. Artifacts and images on the facing wall chronicle the lives of three important Iroquois chiefs—Red Jacket, Joseph Brant, and Handsome Lake—and outline the

British and American colonists presented silver gorgets like these to leaders of the Iroquois peoples as diplomatic gifts of respect.

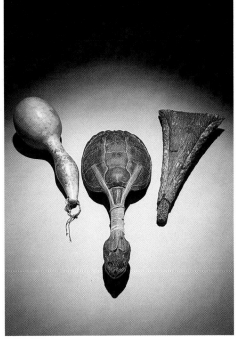

The people of the Iroquois longhouse religion used rattles like these in dances and ceremonies of healing.

steady erosion of Iroquois power and territory under the pressure of white settlers. Opening the Seneca section is the first of the exhibition's two study galleries, which hold changing, in-depth treatments of aspects of the 18th century, such as British ceramics in Maryland and the influence of the Enlightenment on the men who held the reins of power.

The next section offers a glimpse of the daily lives of the merchant Samuel Colton and his family of Longmeadow, Massachusetts. A period room, a tall case clock, silver-ware, and other furnishings represent the kinds of objects that a man of Col-ton's station might have owned and used. Across from the room are the kinds of goods Colton sold in his store: dishes and drinking vessels, shoe buckles, knitting needles, and lace, all imported from Britain; axe-heads, a bed warmer, coarse red earthenware dishes, and other objects made in America.

In 1790 Philadelphia was the coun-try's largest city, its principal seaport, the leading banking and commercial center, and the federal capital. The last and largest section of the exhibi-tion explores this metropolis and its people. A large room is filled with the tools and products of blacksmiths, cabinetmakers, silversmiths, dress-makers, and several other artisans. The exhibition ends with a conclu-sion, a performance space, and the Hands On History Room, a learning center for visitors of all ages. Here

The tools and products of a late 18th-century silversmith.

children can learn what possessions a child of 200 years ago might have had, adults can try on reproductions of 18th-century clothing, and anyone can try the tricky task of putting together a wooden bucket called a "piggin."

THIRD FLOOR

Hall of Ceramics
Potters around the globe have been turning out their everyday wares for millennia. Fine ceramics, however, such as hard-paste porcelain, are more recent innovations, especially in Europe. Chinese and Japanese porcelain imported to Europe in the 17th and 18th centuries inspired an explosion of enthusiasm among wealthy Europeans. At the beginning of this hall, examples of European and Oriental porcelain are displayed side by side, filling several cases; the intricate designs of prunus and bamboo trees, exotic birds, tigers, squirrels, and landscapes stretch across plates, bowls, vases, teacups, even the handles of flatware.

Much of the beauty of the wares from the East lay in the hard-paste porcelain they were made of. European potters searched in vain for the secret of hard-paste porcelain until 1709, when Johann Böttger, an alchemist in Germany, discovered the formula while trying to make gold. At Meissen, Böttger produced both his

This Japanese Imari nine-sided porcelain plate of about 1720 is part of the magnificent Hans Syz Collection of European and Oriental ceramics.

A faience lion made in Luneville, France, about 1740–50.

A Wedgwood earthenware chestnut basket from late 18th-century England.

A molded pitcher with a brown Rockingham-type glaze, produced by the Salamander Works in New York, about 1850.

newly discovered hard-paste porcelain and hard red stoneware. Exhibits trace the history of Meissen porcelain.

The secret of making "true" porcelain was not kept very long. The Vienna factory of Claudius Du Paquier was producing hard-paste porcelain as early as 1719, after having lured two knowledgeable workers from Meissen. A long display case in the next gallery presents products of this Austrian factory and its successors from 1719 to 1810. Dishes, tankards, cups, and figures from German factories fill the rest of the room. Just inside the next gallery, an alcove features products of the *hausmalerai*, artists who took blank pieces of porcelain from the Meissen factory and painted them at home. Also on display here are hard- and soft-paste porcelain from Italy, Spain, Holland, Belgium, Switzerland, Denmark, Germany, and Poland.

Through the next arch are English ceramics, including early examples of English soft-paste wares, from mid-18th-century factories at Bow, Derby, and Chelsea. French porcelain appears in a separate alcove devoted to wares from famous factories in St. Cloud, Sevres, and Paris. Around the corner, a bay contains yellow-glazed British earthenware made from 1785 to 1835 and today called "canary yellow."

Beyond are examples of the work of other English Staffordshire potters, Josiah Wedgwood foremost among them. English transfer-printed earthenware with American views is also shown. A small gallery near the English ceramics holds a collection of decorative tiles—from 12th-century

Persia to modern examples from England, Europe, and America.

The display of American ceramics begins with a stoneware mug of 1773 and a flask of 1789, an 1804 stoneware jar from Boston, and an earthenware teapot and jar of the early 19th century. Early examples of American porcelain from 1770 to 1830 are next to commercial wares of 1850 to 1900, when American manufactories began to produce larger quantities of table and ornamental wares. Other cases present American 19th-century Rockingham wares, a type of molded pottery with a mottled brown glaze, including examples from the well-known Fenton pottery of Bennington, Vermont. American Rockwood and Tiffany art pottery of the late 19th and early 20th centuries is also on display. In a final section is elegant modern studio pottery, largely American, by pioneer artists such as Charles Harden and Charles Fegus Binns and more recent examples by potters such as Nancee Meeker and Warren McKenzie.

Hall of Musical Instruments

"Violin Treasures" presents instruments made by four of the finest craftsmen of stringed instruments, Gaspero de Sallo de Brescia, Niccolo Amati, Giuseppe Guarnieri, and, most famous of all, Antonio Stradivari. All of these makers lived and worked in northern Italy between the mid-16th and mid-18th centuries and produced generations of violins, violas, and violoncellos unsurpassed before or since.

A porcelain vase and cover made in 1910 by the renowned American art potter Adelaide Alsop Robineau.

Antonio Stradivari made this violoncello in Cremona, Italy, in 1701; it has influenced the sound and design of stringed instruments ever since. Perhaps the best-preserved of all of Stradivari's cellos, this instrument is named the "Servais" after its most illustrious owner, the famous 19th-century Belgian cellist Adrien François Servais.

Eighteenth-century musical instruments in the Museum's collections.

The renowned Polish pianist Ignacy Jan Paderewski used this Steinway grand piano on his 1892–93 concert tour of the United States. Paderewski autographed the piano on the soundboard.

Instruments on display include the "Servais" violoncello, made by Stradivari in 1701; an Amati violin of 1675; and the Dr. Herbert Axelrod Stradivari Quartet: two violins, a viola, and a violoncello made by the master between 1687 and 1709.

Just beyond these treasures are other instruments of the 18th and 19th centuries, including a bass viola da gamba made in London in 1718; orchestral kettledrums, probably German, from 1750–75; and many others.

Keyboard instruments at the end of the hall include a 1710 spinet from London; a grand piano, possibly from Munich, of 1790–1800; a square piano made in Philadelphia in 1798; and a Chickering grand piano made in Boston in 1865. The Museum's keyboard instruments are far too numerous to be displayed simultaneously, but a videodisk presentation on the history of the piano allows interested visitors to take a look at many pianos in the collections.

The corridor adjacent to the video-disk kiosk is used for changing displays, featuring important segments of the collection. Recent short-term exhibits have ranged from "Music-Making Country Style," showing banjos, folk violins, and dulcimers, to "Tuning Up: Fiddles and Bass Viols in America," "American Violin Makers before 1830," and selected keyboard instruments from the United States and abroad.

Between these two sections of the Hall of Musical Instruments lies what might be called the heart of the hall—a performance area. Instruments on display and regularly put to work here include a 1761 chamber organ from London, an 18th-century harpsichord from London, and a harpsichord made in Paris in 1760 with a lavishly decorated lid and case. This performance space is regularly the scene of concerts of classical, romantic, and baroque music. In recent years, music from popular and ethnic traditions has also been performed, ranging from bagpipes to gypsy music and contemporary music of Chick Corea and the Beatles. For information on upcoming music programs at the National Museum of American History, call (202) 357-2700; TDD (202) 357-1729.

Hall of the History of Money and Medals

The central section of this hall follows the evolution of money in America from barter on the frontier—where settlers traded in beaver skins and wampum—to 20th-century coins and bills. One exhibit even describes 18th-century exchange rates for wampum: 360 white beads = 5 shillings; 6 white beads = 1 penny.

Coins and paper money issued by various states, the Continental currency of the Revolutionary War era, and early coins from the U.S. Mint, established in 1791, are all displayed here. Further exhibits describe the founding of a national currency, the gold rushes of Georgia and California, the money of the Confederate States

An Athenian owl on a tetradrachmon, struck in Athens, Greece, in the 5th century B.C.

78

A head of liberty pattern for a $50 United States gold piece of 1877, never issued.

of America, and the birth of the Federal Reserve system in 1913. There are additional displays of paper money and gold and silver coins from the 18th to the 20th centuries, including a 1934 $100,000 gold certificate, the largest U.S. denomination ever issued.

Leading to the historical exhibits of American bills and coins are several panels describing the evolution of money of the world from ancient times to the present. Here are the oldest known coins, from Lydia in Asia Minor, struck in the seventh century B.C., and other Greek coins as well as those from the Roman and Byzantine empires. In the eighth century A.D. Charlemagne's monetary reform established the penny. Archduke Sigismund of Tyrol in 1486 gave us the ancestor of the dollar, an example of which is exhibited here.

Nearby displays present selections of exquisite ancient Japanese coins given to President Ulysses S. Grant in 1881; Russian coins and medals equaled only by the collections in Leningrad; and silver multiple talers produced in 17th-century Germany from the Paul A. Straub Collection. The magnificent Josiah K. Lilly Collection fills a gallery of its own with gold coins from North and South America, Europe, and Asia, spanning the centuries from ancient Greek times to the present. The collection includes a virtually complete set of U.S. gold coins. The foreign coins include an excellent series of portrait pieces of the Roman emperors; two 100-ducat pieces, sometimes called the world's largest gold coins; and one of the world's most extensive collections of Latin American gold coins.

These xigui, *a type of hoe or ax blade, and cocoa beans were used as money in early Mexico.*

A side gallery delves into money-less economies around the world. On the Yap Islands of the western Pacific an argonite stone called *rai* served as a medium of exchange. The Yap coin of the realm displayed here is a doughnut-shaped rock more than two feet in diameter. Larger ones on the islands could measure more than six feet across. In parts of Africa, copper rings, hair from elephants' tails, wrought-iron bars, shells, and knives have served as money, and all are presented here. Examples from the Americas include various items such as fishhooks, cocoa beans, and clam shell beads.

Throughout the hall, exhibits show advances in coining techniques over the centuries from hand-hammering to a reproduction of a coin stamper designed by Leonardo da Vinci to 19th-century cast-iron screw presses. A Children's Corner contains a wishing well, dioramas on buried treasure, and money to touch. One corridor leading to the hall introduces the history of gold, silver, and copper mining from earliest times to the California gold rush. The other offers many splendid medals and decorations awarded by governments, religious orders, and other organizations, such as the Order of the Knights of Malta, the Order of the Garter from England, and France's Legion of Honor.

A proof for a $5 note, printed about 1860 by the Monongahela Valley Bank of McKeesport, Pennsylvania.

Early cameras, 1885–1895.

A period setting re-creates the work of Englishman Roger Fenton, the first professional photojournalist. In 1855 Fenton took a wagonful of equipment to what is now part of the Soviet Union to photograph the Crimean War.

The first U.S. Secret Service "mug" book, 1888–89.

Hall of Photography

The fundamentals of photography are centuries old. By the 11th century experimenters had mastered the art of forming images in a box called a camera obscura. At the entrance to this hall a 1646 illustration of the workings of a camera obscura stands near an 1875 patent model that uses the principles of this type of image formation. By the 17th century, scientists had begun to experiment with various chemicals sensitive to light. In the 19th century the work of three men brought these two streams of invention together in modern photography.

In 1826 Joseph Nicéphore Niepce

of France made the first photograph. A reproduction of one of his fuzzy images hangs here. In a short-lived partnership, Niepce worked with another pioneer of photography, Louis Jacques Mandé Daguerre, who in 1839 announced the daguerreotype process, examples of which appear throughout the hall.

At about the same time, across the English Channel, William Henry Fox Talbot introduced the concept of photographic negatives for making positive paper prints. Some of the equipment Talbot used is displayed, including a camera of about 1836 and several chemical bottles. A period set-

A Technicolor camera and dolly of the 1930s.

ting re-creates his photographic laboratory of 1837. Talbot owned and used much of the furniture and photographic equipment displayed here. Close to this area is an exhibit containing a daguerreotype camera, a plate holder, and developing box of 1839 that belonged to the inventor of the telegraph, Samuel F. B. Morse. Above this equipment hangs an 1848 daguerreotype of Daguerre.

Other exhibits in the hall explain the development of wet and dry glass-plate photography and describe the work of pioneers such as Englishmen John Herschel, Robert L. Maddox, and Roger Fenton, the first professional photojournalist. In 1855 Fenton took a wagonful of photographic equipment to the Crimea to record the face of war. A period setting at the entrance of the hall shows Fenton at work, a copy of his wagon, and reproductions of many of his photographs.

Another exhibit deals with the

introduction of commercially prepared gelatin dry plates, an innovation that freed photographers from the necessity of manufacturing their own plates and boosted photography's popularity. It includes a coating device patented in 1880 by George Eastman. A period setting shows workers producing prints from dry plates at the Eastman's Dry Plate and Film Company.

The late 1880s saw the introduction of flexible roll film, which further reduced the bulk and bother of photography, and the first Kodak camera, which incorporated an approach that dramatically encouraged the spread of photography. Several displays and a slide show explore the rise of the amateur photographer here and abroad.

In 1861, just over two decades after Talbot and Daguerre developed their photographic processes, the English scientist James Clerk Maxwell demonstrated how photography can be used to produce images in color. The exhibit area featuring color includes an early color projector and one of the first color pictures. A slide show illustrates the history of color photography and discusses the work of other pioneers in the field.

Cameras from a disposable paper model of 1900 to a Kodak Brownie Starmatic of 1962 are used to illustrate the evolution of cameras for the amateur. Lenses from 1838 on include several by the famous German maker Zeiss as well as early telephoto and zoom lenses. The many ingenious

examples of miniature cameras for reporting and espionage include a camera in the heel of a shoe and another in a cigarette lighter. Flash pistols of 1888, a flashgun and flash powder of about 1930, and many examples of flashbulbs document the history of artificial lighting. Other displays examine the evolution of shutters and light meters, microfilm, stereoscopic photography, xerography, and panoramic photography, which includes a series of photographs some 10 feet long capturing the partially completed Washington Monument in about 1875.

Motion pictures, too, receive a fair share of attention. Objects and labels in this section of the hall describe the work of pioneers in the photographic study of motion, such as France's Étienne J. Marey and an Englishman who immigrated to America, Eadweard Muybridge. Several early devices that create the illusion of movement are also on display, including a toy zoetrope of 1867 and a phenakistoscope of 1832. A replica of a Kinetoscope and several Mutoscopes show the kinds of "peep-show" viewers popular in amusement arcades at the turn of the century. A huge Technicolor camera of the 1930s, and other artifacts introduce the history of the motion-picture industry.

The final galleries of the Hall of Photography explore the uses of the camera in science and discovery. Featured are a deep-sea camera designed by Dr. Harold Edgerton and used in 1954 by the renowned underwater

Jacques-Yves Cousteau first used this deep-sea camera in 1954. It can withstand pressures of 20,000 pounds per square inch.

explorer Jacques-Yves Cousteau, a high-speed Edgerton camera used to photograph early atomic bomb explosions, and a slide show illustrating applications of photography from identification photographs to the eerie realm of the infinitesimal, brought back by electron microscopy.

Hall of Textiles
The Smithsonian's textile collection consists of about 50,000 items, dating from the 17th century to the present time. Besides fabrics and fibers, the collection includes full-size textile machinery and implements as well as patent models of textile-related inventions. Among the latter are historic machines like Samuel Slater's spinning frame and carding machine of the 1790s; an original model of an Eli Whitney cotton gin made by the inventor in the early 1800s; and significant patent models, such as those of Elias Howe's and Isaac Singer's sewing machines.

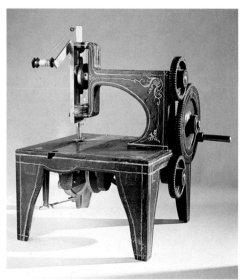

Isaac Singer submitted this model of a sewing machine to the U.S. Patent Office in 1854 to earn a patent for improvements in powering the feed and controlling the needle's thread tension.

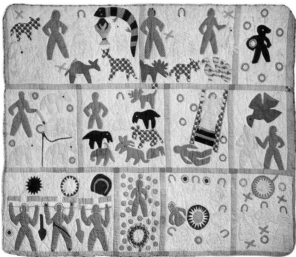

Above: A pieced and embroidered throw, commonly called a "crazy quilt." This late 19th-century piece and many others are part of the Museum's quilt collection. **Bottom photo:** Harriet Powers of Clark County, Georgia, sewed this "Bible Quilt" in about 1886. It depicts the stories of Adam and Eve, Cain and Abel, and several others.

Textile processing devices such as spinning wheels and looms that were used in America during the 18th and 19th centuries are displayed and sometimes demonstrated here. They illustrate the steps housewives or local artisans followed when transforming raw natural fibers, like wool and flax, into bed covers, sheeting, tablecloths, and other household goods. A treadle loom is set up for weaving geometric-patterned bed coverlets, and a floral medallion-patterned tablecloth is being woven on the mid-19th-century loom equipped with a Jacquard punched-card control mechanism. Both types of equipment continued to be used side by side in America until nearly the end of the last century.

The coverlets exhibited represent products of both types of looms. Almost all the coverlets have woven dates, which range from 1784 to 1846. The Museum's collection is especially rich in rare dated and initialed overshot-weave coverlets produced on treadle looms; the majority of 18th- and 19th-century overshot coverlets found today were left undated by their anonymous weavers. The 1846-dated tablecloth in the display provided the pattern for the cloth being woven on the Jacquard-equipped loom. An 1824-dated coverlet with a similar pattern is proof that the design was popular enough to be used for over 20 years. The same craftsmen who wove such tablecloths also wove the coverlets; in addition, many produced the double-layered, flat, reversible carpeting known as ingrain, or Scotch, carpeting.

The ladies' shawls, popularly known as "paisleys," were made on the Jacquard-equipped looms. While few were made in the United States, many were imported to this country from weaving centers in France, Germany, Austria, England, and especially Paisley, Scotland, whose name is still applied to designs similar to those found on the 19th-century shawls.

The most impressive object in the Textile Hall is the 13 ½ foot-high Jacquard punched-card-controlled loom. The Jacquard device, which rests on top of an ordinary handloom base, was introduced in France in 1804 by Joseph Marie Jacquard, a Lyon silk weaver-turned-inventor. His mechanism was the earliest application of punched cards to control a manufacturing process. It enabled an unassisted weaver to produce complicated woven-patterned fabrics automatically. It also gave Charles Babbage, a 19th-century mathematician, the idea of using punched cards to program the calculating machine that he was developing in the 1830s; and indirectly it may have inspired Herman Hollerith to utilize punched cards with the machine he devised for tabulating the 1890 census figures.

Such developments in the textile industries of the United States and other countries suggest that this industry has had—and continues to have—a great influence on the lives and well-being of peoples all over the globe.

A Wells press, built in Hartford, Connecticut, by John I. Wells about 1820. This press introduced a simple toggle mechanism for making the impression, an innovation widely copied among American iron hand presses.

Hall of Printing and Graphic Arts

At the heart of this hall are printing presses, patent models, and illustrations that show the evolution of printing. These include an 1819 Wells press; an 1820 press built by Adam Ramage, the best-known early American press builder; an 1850 "Philadelphia" press; and an 1865 Columbian press.

Models show improvements in the cylinder press, introduced in the

United States by R. Hoe and Company of New York in the 1830s. A Hoe "Railway" cylinder press of about 1860 and a one-revolution cylinder press of about 1879, which together drove the 19th-century book and newspaper trade, are also on display. An illustration shows the gigantic 10-cylinder Hoe "Lightning" rotary press, the type used by the London *Daily Telegraph* and other newspapers after about 1860. Presses like this could print 20,000 sheets an hour and dramatically increased newspaper circulations.

Just after the turn of the century, American inventors Ira Rubel and the brothers Charles and Albert Harris independently developed offset printing, a technique widely used today. A Rubel offset press of 1905 and a Harris press stand near one end of the hall. The same platform holds a half-scale model of the Nicolas–Louis Robert papermaking machine, recently built from his drawings of 1800. Modern papermaking machinery is based on Robert's concept.

Beyond the offset presses, in the printmaking corner, exhibits describe the techniques of etching, woodcutting, lithography, photoengraving, collotype, and other processes. The displays feature many fine old master and modern prints.

Around the presses and prints, the graphic arts come to life in four shops—three print shops and a typefoundry. The typefoundry is an 1850s re-creation where demonstrations show how type was created mechanically or by hand. A page from a Bible printed in the 15th century by Johan Gutenberg, the inventor of printing with moveable type, adorns the wall outside the shop. Ranging down the wall from the typefounding shop is a row of typesetting machines beginning with American inventor Ottmar Merganthaler's Second Band Machine of 1885 and a Blower Linotype of 1890. Both were precursors of his famous Linotype machine, which revolutionized the printing industry by allowing typesetters to cast entire lines of type without much more

The job printing shop (foreground) and the type foundry, which features regular demonstrations, are two of the shops in the Hall of Graphic Arts.

In the printmaking corner, exhibits describe etching, woodcutting, lithography, and several other printing processes.

The newspaper office period room shows the printing presses and type that many small town newspapers might have used well into the 20th century.

effort than striking the keys of a typewriter.

Beyond the typesetting machines is a re-creation of a newspaper office of about 1885. It houses a steam-driven Hoe drum cylinder press to print the newspaper, a platen job press for smaller jobs, and the type cases and frames found in every small printer's or newspaperman's shop of the day.

Around the corner is a job print shop of about 1860, where a printer would have earned a living from a stream of broadsides, billheads, and announcements. This shop contains a Washington press—the most widely used press in 19th-century America—a Gordon "Firefly" press of 1852, and a Ruggles card-and-billhead press of 1851. The last shop in the hall is the oldest, a re-created print shop and post office of the early 19th century. Inside are a rebuilt common press of about 1815 used in the United States and the "Franklin" press, on which Benjamin Franklin may have worked as a printer's apprentice in England in 1726. All four shops feature either regular or occasional demonstrations. Call (202) 357-2877, Monday through Friday, for days and times. For additional information ask at the information desks or call Smithsonian Information at (202) 357-2700; TDD (202) 357-1729.

Hall of Postal History and Philately
Outside the print shop and post office at the entrance of the Hall of Postal History and Philately, Benjamin Franklin greets a colonial postrider.

Two hundred and fifty years ago he might have given the rider a copy of his newspaper, the *Pennsylvania Gazette.* The hall goes on to present the history of the mails both in America and around the world and to explore the creation, collection, history, and fun of stamps.

Exhibits of U.S. postal history examine such subjects as the Pony Express, city delivery, parcel post, railway mail service, special delivery, rural free delivery, and the birth of the U.S. Airmail Service. Objects on display include mail pouches, uniforms, postal scales, mailboxes, and postal vehicles, including a 1931 Ford Model AA mail truck. Scores of canceled stamps and letters from around the world and illustrations of dozens of 19th- and 20th-century American post offices complement the exhibition.

A large central section of the hall is devoted to "The Mails and Speed in America," which records the history of mail delivery and improvements in both carrying and handling the mails. Objects on display include canceling machines, meter machines, a pneumatic tube mail carrier used in New York City, many household mailboxes and lamppost letterboxes, and manufacturers' models of vehicles purchased by the U.S. Postal Service in years past to deliver the mail. Special panels on "The Perils of the Posts" describe mail-coach robberies, shipwrecks, train wrecks and robberies, and airmail plane crashes.

The hall also describes the interna-

This 1904-style screen wagon was used to move mail from post offices to railway depots and steamboat landings in about 100 cities. This type of wagon was introduced in 1886 in Sherman, Texas.

A replica of a Sumerian message tablet, written in cuneiform, of about 2500 to 2150 B.C.

tional history of mail service over the last 5,000 years. Exhibits here include reproductions of Sumerian messages on clay tablets, which may have been the first letters; an unopened Egyptian papyrus letter; 18th- and 19th-century letters carried by the Italian private courier service of Thurn and Taxis; and other displays on the national postal systems of Europe, including that of Great Britain, where the adhesive postage stamp was invented in about 1840.

Lining the walls are some 470 pullout frames holding roughly 75,000 stamps from around the globe, a mere fraction of the 10 million or so stamps in the care of the National Philatelic Collection. Here are exquisite miniature works of art, from Aden to Lithuania to Zululand. Between the two rows of stamps is a corner of exhibits that reveals how stamps are produced—from the artwork and engraving stages to platemaking and perforating.

Budding stamp collectors will find the several panels on the specialized language of philately useful. Here examples of stamps and descriptive labels explain terms such as *perfin, precancel,* and *backstamp* amid broader discussions of paper, watermarks, adhesives, stamp classifications, postal markings, and other aspects of philately.

Collectors should also be sure to see the changing exhibit of philatelic rarities, which includes a 1918 24-cent airmail stamp with a biplane flying upside down (fewer than 100 of these

In the 19th century, the national government acknowledged payment of taxes on many commodities by issuing Internal Revenue stamps. This $5,000 stamp, nicknamed the "Persian Rug" for its color and design, was approved but never issued.

George Washington used this camp chest during the Revolutionary War. The uniform dates from after the conflict.

The gunboat Philadelphia *is the oldest surviving American fighting vessel. Built in 1776, it was sunk in Lake Champlain during an American victory over the British in the same year. The popular "1776" demonstration center is adjacent to the gunboat.*

stamps exist), a letter carried by the Pony Express, and many other unique items.

Hall of Armed Forces History
Military artifacts from the French and Indian War to the end of the Civil War are the major attractions of this hall. At the entrance, a uniform worn by George Washington, a portion of his headquarter's tent, his camp mess chest, and a spyglass survive here as reminders of the American Revolution. A trophy cannon from the crucial battle of Saratoga, shoes, uniforms, a saddle, a book of drill regulations, a sword carried by the French Count de Rochambeau, and scores of other artifacts trace the history of the struggle from Lexington and Concord to final victory at Yorktown.

Both the Navy and the Continental

The flag of the 84th Regiment, U.S. Colored Infantry, which fought in many campaigns of the Civil War in Louisiana and Texas.

Marines were disbanded after the Revolutionary War, only to be reborn a decade later to combat the French in the undeclared naval war of 1798. Scale models show the 38-gun frigate *Constellation* and the 44-gun *Constitution* (affectionately remembered as "Old Ironsides"), both commissioned to counter French privateers. These vessels and their complements of Marines fought the French in the Caribbean, the Barbary pirates off the coast of North Africa, and the British during the War of 1812. Displays on the Marines of the period show swords, epaulettes, and an example of the high leather collar worn by Marines until 1875 that led to their nickname "leathernecks."

Although the nation at war is a main theme of this hall, many dis-plays deal with noncombat experiences of American citizen-soldiers. These range from exhibits describing the engineering of seagoing vessels and the educational role of the U.S. Military Academy in training engineers to the mid-century voyages of exploration carried out by Commodores James Biddle and Matthew Perry to the mysterious land of Japan.

In the Mexican War, between 1846 and 1848, young officers like Ulysses S. Grant, Robert E. Lee, and Thomas J. "Stonewall" Jackson fought together in Mexico. Later Lee and Jackson would confront Grant and others in the bitter battles of the American Civil War. In addition to many American artifacts, the exhibits also present a Mexican uniform, battle flag, and battle implements.

Curator Harold Langley examines "Old Glory" before the flag was conserved and put on display. Captain William Driver raised this flag over the Tennessee state capitol in Nashville on February 25, 1862, to signify the liberation of the city by Union troops during the Civil War. "Old Glory," Driver's private term for the flag, became a nickname for the American flag.

In the closing months of the Civil War, General Philip Sheridan rode this horse, named "Rienzi" and later renamed "Winchester," to the town of Winchester in northwestern Virginia to turn a potential defeat for the Union forces into a victory.

Much of the remaining space in the Hall of Armed Forces History describes the Civil War, our nation's deadliest, most costly conflict, since virtually every casualty was an American. The weapons, uniforms, and related equipment of soldiers blue and gray are on display.

This section of the hall also contains a few unusual artifacts. One is Winchester, the horse General Philip Sheridan rode down the Shenandoah Valley to the city of that name in northwestern Virginia to rally his troops and turn a potential defeat for U.S. Army forces into a victory. Another is a case entitled "The Soldier and His Stomach" that describes the soldier's diet and displays a mess kit, a coffee can, tobacco, and an example of the thin, flat, dry, tough biscuit that sustained most soldiers throughout the war—hardtack.

The last gallery is devoted to the evolution of naval technology, from the sailing ship *Falkland* to the Polaris submarine, *George Washington*.

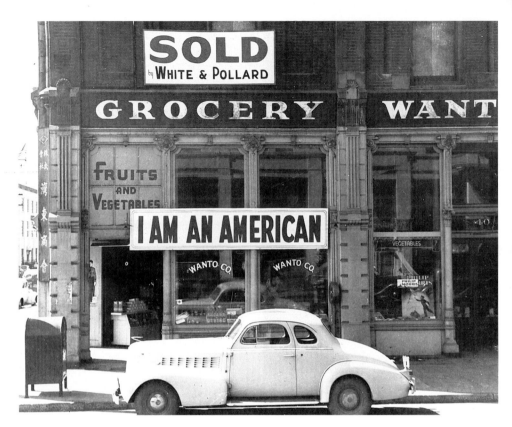

This store in Oakland, California, was closed following the orders to Japanese Americans to leave their homes. The owner, a graduate of the University of California, placed the "I am an American" sign on his storefront on December 8, 1941, the day after the Japanese attack on Pearl Harbor. Courtesy of the National Japanese American Historical Society.

A More Perfect Union: Japanese Americans and the United States Constitution

The Constitution was drafted in only 16 weeks in 1787 by men now revered in American history, including George Washington, Benjamin Franklin, and James Madison. *A More Perfect Union*, an exhibition in one-half of the Hall of Armed Forces History, celebrates the Constitution but goes on to reveal how in a time of grave national crisis, racial fear and prejudice swept away the freedoms it guarantees.

During the opening months of World War II, almost 120,000 Japanese Americans, two-thirds of them citizens of the United States, were forced to leave their homes, sell much of their property at enormous losses, and move into detention camps. The act that made this detention possible was Executive Order 9066, issued by President Franklin Roosevelt on February 19, 1942. In the entrance area to this exhibition, before a mural of photographs showing the process of incarcerating Japanese Americans, a

A mother and sleeping baby ready to leave their home on Bainbridge Island, Washington, for a temporary assembly center, March 30, 1942. Courtesy of the National Japanese American Historical Society.

The Japanese attack on Pearl Harbor on December 7, 1941, sparked a fire of racial prejudice that would quickly drive Japanese-Americans into the camps. In just over a month, the West Coast had been divided into military areas that could exclude citizens under the terms of Executive Order 9066. The Wartime Civil Control Administration was quickly established to supervise the relocation. Several early evacuation orders and public proclamations are preserved here.

The next section of the exhibition examines detention itself: registration, the forced sale of property, and the camps. Inmates' possessions, such as footlockers, duffel bags, and suitcases, as well as scores of photographs of assembly centers, families clutching their belongings, and other scenes, illustrate the beginnings of internment.

copy of the order and an early draft of the Constitution rest side by side. Through displays of hundreds of photographs and everyday objects, the exhibition traces the immigration of Japanese to the mainland of the United States and to Hawaii. The rising power of Japan in the early decades of the 20th century increased fear and prejudice toward Japanese Americans. Newspaper headlines of the period on display cry out warnings to America: "No Japs in Our Schools" and "Japan Demands Vast Sphere in East Asia and South Seas."

A warning sign from the detention camp at Manzanar, California.

Above photo: Campaign pamphlets, a Thompson .45-caliber sub-machine gun, and unit patches from the 100th Infantry Battalion/442nd Regimental Combat Team, a Japanese-American unit that fought in Europe during World War II. ***Bottom photo:*** *A helmet, medic's arm-band, and decorations (from left to right a silver star, an Italian cross, and a purple heart). The 100th/442nd was the most decorated American military unit of its size in World War II.*

A re-creation of a typical barracks room at a detention camp is the centerpiece of the exhibition. The room is based on drawings of a barracks at the Jerome, Arkansas, camp. All of the furnishings inside—from a washboard to a Japanese lantern—were made or used in the camps. Photographs of barbed wire and guard towers, flimsy housing, classrooms, Boy Scout troops, even of a beauty pageant and a communion class, capture the sights of the camps. These images supplement the history embodied in newspapers, bulletins, sketchbooks, wood carvings, jewelry, vases, clothing, and furniture owned or made by internees. An interactive videodisk program allows visitors to learn about the experience of evacuation and detention in the words of men and women imprisoned in the camps.

Public Proclamation Number 21, issued on December 17, 1944, announced that all of the camps would be closed within a year. The inmates left gradually; each received $25 with which to begin his or her life again. Outside, some were welcomed home by old neighbors; some had no homes to return to; others faced the same prejudice that had created the camps. Newspaper headlines of 1944 and 1945 document these mixed reactions: "Mayor Gives Greeting to Japanese Americans" and "Madera Night-Riders Fire into Home of Nisei War Veteran."

Although the closing of the camps might seem to signal the end of the

General Mark Clark, the Fifth Army Commander, reviews the troops of the Japanese-American 100th Infantry Battalion before a decoration ceremony in Leghorn, Italy, August 1944. Courtesy of the National Japanese American Historical Society.

story, an important part remains. Approximately 33,000 American citizens of Japanese ancestry, men and women, served in the U.S. military during the war. The most famous were members of the 100th Battalion/442nd Regimental Combat Team, a group composed almost entirely of Japanese Americans from Hawaii and the detention camps, and the most decorated American unit of its size in the war. Several of the decorations, including a Congressional Medal of Honor, are on display. A 105mm howitzer, a jeep, the original unit flags of the 100th Battalion and 442nd Regimental Combat Team, and other artifacts document the unit's history. Photographs of Italy, France, and Germany detail the soldiers' fight across Europe. Another videodisk program allows visitors to ask for information about selected artifacts in the displays.

At war's end, returning soldiers and their families faced another challenge—finding a way back into a society that had spurned them. Japanese Americans, a people who had refused to give up on themselves or the system, began an effort that continues today to ensure that all Americans recognize the need for each citizen to support and defend the civil liberties guaranteed in the Constitution. In so doing, they have moved all of us a step closer to the "More Perfect Union" envisioned by the nation's founders.

A mezzanine above the exhibition holds a study gallery displaying U.S. firearms from the colonial period to the present. The 1776 gunboat *Philadelphia*, the oldest American fighting vessel in existence, is also displayed nearby.

The Jacksonville Bandstand on the Museum's west grounds, shown here during its opening ceremonies on July 4, 1984, is the scene of regular open-air summer concerts.

OTHER PROGRAMS AND SERVICES

Public Programs The Museum offers a wide variety of regular programs, demonstrations, and concerts designed to bring the public closer to the Museum's collections and exhibitions. These include: a regular Saturday After Noon series of lectures, tours, and panel discussions on topics ranging from freedom of the press to gentility in the 18th century; the All-American Music series, which offers a broad range of American music, including classical, jazz, gospel, rhythm and blues, traditional folk, Latin, and other types; the American Sampler series, devoted to dance, storytelling, and music; Palm Court Cameos, featuring turn-of-the-century theater, vaudeville, and popular music; Jazz in the Palm Court, which explores the roots of jazz and blues; and, in the summer, outdoor concerts in the Jacksonville Bandstand on the west grounds. All programs are free and open to the public. The Division of Education produces and staffs many of the demonstrations around the Museum and oversees the activities of hundreds of volunteer docents, who conduct tours for more than 100,000 visitors every year. The division also develops curriculum kits for elementary and secondary American history courses.

The Program in African American Culture produces colloquia, often combined with musical performances, that explore African-American culture to reveal both its uniqueness and its importance to American culture. Past programs have focused on classic gospel song, the evolution of rhythm and blues, the civil rights movement, and many other topics. The program also conducts research and maintains archives open to the public. For more information call (202) 357-4176.

The Division of Musical History also presents regular musical offerings. The Chamber Music Program, which comprises the Smithsonian Chamber Players, the Smithson String Quartet, the Castle Trio, and the Smithsonian Chamber Orchestra, gives some 40 concerts annually, many performed on instruments from the Museum's collections. Their recordings include the six-record set *J. S. Bach,* offered through the Smithsonian Institution Press. Their broadcasts over the National Public Radio and American Public Radio networks have reached more than 10 million people.

For more information about any of the programs above, call (202) 357-2124 Monday through Friday, or Smithsonian Information at (202) 357-2700, TDD (202) 357-1729, seven days a week.

The Archives Center The Archives Center serves the Museum by acquiring collections of documentary materials and historical records and then organizing, preserving, and making them accessible for research. These collections include personal papers, records of businesses and other organizations, historical photographs, films, videotapes, sound recordings, oral histories, and advertising ephem-

The old post office and general store from Headsville, West Virginia, is now a working post office near the Museum's Constitution Avenue entrance.

The National Museum of American History

108

Designed in turn-of-the-century style, the Palm Court offers visitors a place to read, relax, and enjoy musical programs.

The interior of Stohlman's Confectionary Shop, built in Washington, D.C., in about 1900, lines one side of the Palm Court.

era. There are three main program areas: the manuscript collections, the advertising history collections, and the historical photograph collections. The Archives Center is open to researchers Monday through Friday from 10 a.m. to 5 p.m. Researchers are encouraged to contact the Archives Center before their arrival at (202) 357-3270, Monday through Friday, or call Smithsonian Information (202) 357-2700; TDD (202) 357-1729. Address written inquiries to: Archives Center, Room C340, National Museum of American History, Smithsonian Institution, Washington, D.C. 20560.

The Dibner Library This library houses one of the world's foremost collections of rare books on the history of science and technology and attracts scholars and students from around the world. Recent renovations have added an exhibition area and a lounge and offices for approximately 20 Smithsonian Fellows. The Dibner Library is open by appointment only; call (202) 357-1577, Monday through Friday, or Smithsonian Information at (202) 357-2700; TDD (202) 357-1729.